Crime and Cover-Up

Contents

Foreword

Peter Dale Scott has emerged as the unchallenged expert on the political, underworld, and labor union interrelationships in the complex framework of the assassinations in Dallas and elsewhere. His study of the Schweiker-Hart Report and the Dallas-Watergate connection is a small masterpiece which renders understandable a Byzantine picture of internecine rivalries within government agencies and the intelligence apparatus, and the whole shabby interlinkage of conspiracy within conspiracies.

His analysis of the Schweiker-Hart Report throws needed new light on that document and on the busy attempts being made to falsely implicate Fidel Castro in the assassination of President Kennedy. For all its scrupulous scholarship, Scott's study is an exciting and illuminating view of hidden aspects of this country's sinister era of assassination and Watergate. It is a remarkable *tour de force* that reaches compelling verdicts about the present state of the nation and the dangers which still lie ahead.

Sylvia Meagher

New York
December 4, 1976

Preface

In the three months since I began this essay on the assassination of President Kennedy and its aftermath, events have continued to unfold with increasing momentum. One central CIA-Mafia plotter has been assassinated. The identity of an anonymous associate has been revealed. John Dean's account of Watergate has confirmed some of my own interpretation of Nixon White House concern with another associate, Robert Maheu, and through him with Lawrence O'Brien and even Clifford Irving. One of the Cubans involved in anti-Castro plots is now being sought for his role in blowing up a civilian Cuban airliner and killing seventy-three persons. Meanwhile, the House of Representatives has established a committee to investigate the assassinations of both John F. Kennedy and Martin Luther King.

It is encouraging to read that the chief counsel for this committee has envisaged a long and unhurried investigation. I have argued elsewhere that the model for this inquiry should be that of the Watergate Committee: it should begin not with key suspects, but with low-level and relatively innocent figures whose obstruction of justice can be demonstrated, but whose motive may have been no worse than to protect the so-called "national security." Such figures abound in the story of the Kennedy assassination and cover-up; some of them appear briefly in the ensuing pages. Though not designed primarily as an investigative memorandum, this essay attempts to explore the relationships of these persons to official intelligence activities, authorized and unauthorized, and to speculate how these covert intrigues may have been exploited by witting participants to provide immunity from prosecution for their own illicit crimes. In this way it does sketch the rough outline of a trail by which the sworn testimony of marginal low-level persons may lead to central truths still hidden.

The method of this essay is heuristic, exploratory rather than demonstrative, necessarily reticulate rather than linear. The reader should guard against stock responses to emotionally charged terms like "CIA," "Mafia," and "plots": the associations of persons with CIA-Mafia plots against Castro are explored in this essay, not to impute individual guilt, but to see how such plots may have affected the overall conduct of domestic and foreign politics.

Recurrently in the pages which follow, I note how the Warren Commission, four of whose seven members were from Congress, held back from investigating areas which were highly embarrassing, not only to our intelligence establishment, but to both political parties:

> the ... story, because of its high-level political implications, also indicates how difficult it will prove for any congressional committee to take up the work left unfinished by Senators Schweiker and Hart. ... The truth is so relevant, so important, that its very revelation is tantamount to a restructuring of our political process. (p. 46)

These words, written before the announcements about the new House committee, were not offered in a spirit of cynicism, or even what T. S. Eliot once called "uncynical disillusion," but rather out of a faith that can have no room for complacency.

I believe that those who care today about truth, decency, and open politics can, if they choose, prevail over the bureaucratic forces of official murder and conspiratorial politics. As America's future in a rapidly changing world order is not yet clear, so, too, the future of what is symbolized (not very accurately) by "CIA activities" is not yet certain. A historic confrontation that came to divide U.S. politics in the Vietnam War is not yet resolved: America in future will probably be even more conspiratorially interventionist, or else much less so. The choice may be determined in part by the ability of the next Congress to confront the realities of the Kennedy assassination.

That undoubtedly will not be easy. But the very difficulty of the task is no more than a measure of its importance.

Peter Dale Scott

Berkeley, California
October 16, 1976

Acknowledgments

What follows incorporates the research and collaboration of many more people than I can mention here. In particular I would like to thank Russell Stetler, the producer of the book you are reading, also Paul L. Hoch, Betsy Bowden, Charles Hersch, and my recurring indexer Susan Eason.

For assistance and guidance in the past I am again indebted to many. My researches would have been impossible without the varieties of assistance received from Jo Pomerance and the trail-blazing achievements of Sylvia Meagher. I must also thank, among others, Robert Silvers, Josiah Thompson, Richard Popkin, Jones Harris, Harold Weisberg, Bernard Fensterwald, Jim Lesar, and Howard Kohn.

My gratitude to my wife Maylie is different, overwhelming, and beyond expression.

Abbreviations

The following abbreviations have been used in parenthetical citations appearing in the text. Complete publication data for the works identified below will be found in the Notes, beginning on page 51.

SHR = Schweiker-Hart Report

    R = Warren Report (R 788 = Warren Report, page 788)

    H = Warren Commission Hearings (22 H 20 = volume 22 of the Hearings, page 20)

  CD = Warren Commission Document (from the National Archives)

Wat = Ervin Committee Hearings (24 Wat 11663 = volume 24 of the Hearings, page 11663)

Crime and Cover-Up

On June 23, 1976, Senators Richard S. Schweiker and Gary Hart finally released their subcommittee report on the investigation by intelligence agencies of the assassination of President John F. Kennedy. Three weeks earlier the contents of this report had already persuaded the Senate Select Committee on Intelligence Activities to recommend, as its last official act before going out of business, that the new Senate Intelligence Committee "continue this investigation in those areas where the Select Committee's investigation could not be completed." [1]

If it had accomplished nothing else, the Schweiker-Hart Report would have thus earned its place in history. For the first time in a dozen years, an official body had publicly endorsed the belief of an overwhelming majority of Americans—that the findings of the Warren Commission could not be accepted as final. But after this breakthrough, many of the initial press accounts of the report itself may have struck students of the assassination as anti-climactic. News stories suggested that the report focused on tenuous leads to Fidel Castro as the possible assassin, through possible double-agents or uninvestigated Cuban voyagers on mysterious plane flights.

The report itself has a much more serious and irrefutable conclusion, however restrained by the mandated scope of its investigation and by the problems of reaching a bipartisan consensus. That conclusion is that "both the CIA and the FBI failed in, or avoided carrying out, certain of their responsibilities" in the investigation of the assassination (Schweiker-Hart Report, p. 2). As the *Washington Post* paraphrased it the next day, "senior officials of both the CIA and the FBI covered up crucial information" in the course of their investigations. [2] Relevant facts were withheld from both the Warren Commission and "those individuals *within* the FBI and the CIA, as well as other agencies of Government, who were charged with investigating the assassination" (SHR, p. 6, emphasis added).

1

This charge is, of course, only as important as the original facts that were withheld. The subcommittee, charged to examine only the role of the intelligence agencies in the investigation, could thus look at the deficiencies of these agencies only; it could not evaluate the facts of the assassination itself. We believe, however, that a reading of the report as a whole will persuade most readers that the cover-up was not only a conscious obstruction of the investigative process, it was symptomatic of something even more disturbingly wrong within the federal bureaucracy, including deep-rooted factional intrigues antedating the assassination itself. In the context of other facts long known to independent assassination researchers, the report's detailed findings link the documented CIA-Mafia plots against Castro more closely than ever to the context of the John F. Kennedy assassination, including Lee Harvey Oswald's known contacts with anti-Castro Cubans who had worked for the CIA.

Even more important, it suggests that principals in the 1960 CIA-Mafia plot against Castro have continued over the years to use their knowledge of that plot to blackmail the U.S. government—by hinting knowledgeably that it somehow led to the death of President Kennedy. This is perhaps the most important of the Schweiker-Hart revelations, since it suggests an ongoing intrigue involving later internal fights in the Teamsters and Howard Hughes organizations—an intrigue which may have led in the end to Watergate itself. In 1967, as later in 1971, columns by Jack Anderson leaking this story led to significant White House responses, which had direct bearing on powerful internal crises at these precise moments within the Teamster and Howard Hughes organizations, and the Democratic Party. This pattern of blackmail by insiders is not only suggestive of Watergate, but may, as we shall see, have led to the Watergate burglary, whose conspirators figure in almost every phase of the Schweiker-Hart revelations.

These are some of the key new pieces supplied by the Schweiker-Hart Report to the assassination jigsaw puzzle:

(a) FBI officials wrote in 1964 that their "public" position on how the Oswald case had been handled, although justifiable, was not true (p. 54);

(b) Lower-level U.S. officers misleadingly supported a false Oswald story from a secret agent of Nicaragua, a country then actively plotting with the CIA's Cubans (including future Watergate burglars) to overthrow Castro (pp. 28-29);

(c) U.S. "underworld figures" (p. 79) were operating a guerrilla training camp near New Orleans which was being supported by Nicaragua, and assisted by Oswald's chief anti-Castro Cuban contact in New Orleans (p. 12);

(d) One of the Cubans involved in this operation (p. 12) claimed to be a lifelong friend of Rolando Cubela, code-named AMLASH, the Cuban official recruited by the CIA to kill Castro in 1963; this Cuban gave information to the FBI and CIA linking the AMLASH operation to the 1960-62 CIA-Mafia plots against Castro (p. 78);

(e) In 1967 a lawyer for "underworld" people "used by the CIA" in these plots learned from them that "Castro planned Kennedy's assassination" (pp. 80-84, 105), in retaliation for what sounds like the AMLASH plot (pp. 84-85). The lawyer contacted Drew Pearson, and (after instructions from the White House) was interviewed by the FBI.

The Schweiker-Hart Report, in reporting these facts, did not attempt to interpret them. In the following pages I shall argue that the lawyer's underworld sources for the "Castro story"—who have since denied knowing of it (p. 85n)—were using that story with some success as a form of blackmail against the U.S. government. To understand how or why this could be, one must stand back and take a broader look at the interaction between foreign and domestic U.S. political intrigue.

The career of one man in particular will help us to see the various facts reported above as part of a single ominous picture. That man, as we shall see, is Jack Ruby. By piecing together the known facts of Ruby's career, we shall see that the interlocking CIA-Mafia plot against Castro recruited elements from the very highest level of government-criminal collaboration, a grey alliance at work in the Teamsters, in the Hughes casino organization, and in both political parties.

And our study will suggest that, despite the apparent purgations after Watergate, this same baleful influence is still with us today.

Evidence of an Official Cover-Up

The report publishes documentary evidence and testimony that, from as early as the murder of Oswald on November 24, 1963, the primary focus of FBI activity was not to investigate the JFK assassination, but to gather evidence that Oswald was the assassin. A White

House memo of that day quotes J. Edgar Hoover as saying,

> The thing I am most concerned about, and so is [Deputy Attorney General] Katzenbach, is having something issued so we can convince the public that Oswald is the real assassin. (p. 33)

An FBI memo two days later of a subsequent discussion between Hoover and Katzenbach records agreement to issue an FBI report

> to settle the dust, insofar as Oswald and his activities are concerned, both from the standpoint that he is the man who assassinated the President, and relative to Oswald himself and his activities and background. (p. 33)

These two reports then officially document the privately voiced complaint of Warren Commission member Gerald Ford on June 4, 1964 that Katzenbach was pressuring the commission for "a statement to the effect that there was no foreign involvement, there was no conspiracy."[3]

Press accounts on December 3, 1963, that "an exhaustive FBI report ... will indicate that Lee Harvey Oswald was the lone and unaided assassin" are now revealed to have been based on leaks by J. Edgar Hoover himself. Critics have long noted that the same constraints later inhibited the Warren Commission: from the very beginning it, too, investigated not the assassin, but "Lee Harvey Oswald as the assassin." It is clear from a recently declassified transcript of a Warren Commission executive session that the commission's own counsel justified his self-imposed restrictions by pointing to the "difficulty" that the FBI had already "decided that it is Oswald," just as the FBI justified its own restrictions by pointing to the fact that Oswald had already been "formally charged" by the Dallas police.[4]

Hoover's rush to name the assassin publicly was motivated, according to his former assistant William C. Sullivan, by a desire to cut off, or at least circumscribe, an independent inquiry by the Warren Commission. This does not mean that he was satisfied with the FBI's public posture that there were no problems. Quite the contrary; he shared the opinion of his Assistant Director for Inspection James H. Gale that the FBI had much to hide, and he was looking for ways to hide it.

The Schweiker-Hart Report reveals for the first time that FBI Headquarters officials (i.e., in the Domestic Intelligence Division) were censured for their handling of the Oswald case prior to the assassination, including an Assistant Director (William C. Sullivan), and above him one of the two Assistants to the Director (Alan H. Belmont, who resigned one year later). As Gale reported in December 1963,

> Oswald should have been on the Security Index [the FBI's list of potential subversives for detention in case of a political emergency]; his wife should have been interviewed before the assassination, and investigation intensified—not held in abeyance—after Oswald contacted Soviet Embassy in Mexico. (p. 50)

When Alan Belmont (the Assistant to the Director responsible for the Index) suggested that one should redefine the criteria for the Index, "rather than take the position that all these employees were mistaken," Hoover's response was vehement: "They were worse than mistaken. Certainly no one in full possession of all his faculties can claim Oswald didn't fall within this [sic] criteria." (p. 51)

In a general way, this division within the FBI reflected the growing disagreement about the current danger of the internal Communist threat between Hoover and William Sullivan, who, reflecting his years of collaboration with other like-minded government agencies, had begun to voice public doubts from as early as 1961 (the year he became Assistant Director for Domestic Intelligence) that the Communist danger was as great as the FBI had claimed.[5] Noting this difference, the John Birch Society had attacked Sullivan in the November 1963 issue of *American Opinion:*

> When the Assistant Director of the FBI starts sounding like Robert McNamara, Earl Warren, and Dean Rusk all rolled into one, we begin to wonder about the future of the FBI.

That Sullivan should sound more like the rest of the government is not surprising. His division included the branch responsible for liaison with other intelligence agencies, including the CIA. At least it did so until 1970, when Hoover finally abolished the liaison branch altogether. This provoked President Richard Nixon, with the aid of Sullivan, to propose the ill-starred Huston Plan for White House coordination of domestic intelligence, which was exposed through Watergate.

Internal Conflicts Over the Oswald Case

More specifically, however, Hoover appears to have intervened personally in the Oswald case from as early as 1960,[6] when he checked up on the unconcerned way in which it had been handled by the rest of the government—along with the FBI's Domestic Intelligence Division under first Belmont and then Sullivan. We learn now that Inspector Gale disagreed when his superior Alan H. Belmont assured the Warren Commission that Oswald's activities "did not warrant" the ordering of a "look-out card" on Oswald in the State Department, to alert the FBI to his activities. Gale went on to suggest that the valid reason for withholding such a card would have been Oswald's intelligence assignments:

> Inspector feels it was proper at that time to take this [i.e., Belmont's] "public" position. However, it is felt that with Oswald's background we should have had a stop [look-out card] on his passport, particularly since we did not know definitely whether or not he had any intelligence assignments at that time. (p. 54)

Logically, Gale's judgment must refer to *U.S.* intelligence assignments, the only assignments which could have mitigated, rather than strengthened, the need to keep track of Oswald's movements. The adverbial qualifiers (*definitely . . . at that time*) suggest that the FBI had been receiving indefinite intimations that Oswald at some time had had such assignments. This indeed was the firm conviction of Oswald's mother, a fact which a Washington agent added discordantly to the otherwise complacent FBI files on Oswald (it would appear from the files that no one was ever asked by the FBI about this possibility). An official of at least one other agency also reportedly assumed that Oswald "was employed by the government in some capacity in Russia."[7] This official, E. S. Thurman (22 H 20), was never questioned by the Warren Commission.

The Warren Commission was concerned that quite apart from the FBI, the State Department appeared to have violated—as many as three times—its own clear instructions which called for the issuance of a look-out card on Lee Harvey Oswald.[8] Apparently no such card was ever issued, perhaps because the responsibility for doing so (as long as Oswald was out of the country) lay with that part of the Passport Office (the Foreign Operations Division) which maintained liaison with the CIA.

As early as June 1960 Hoover personally involved himself in the Oswald case, by sending a letter to the FBI's watchdog group inside the State Department, the Office of Security. In that letter Hoover noted that, according to Oswald's mother, Oswald "had taken his birth certificate with him when he left" (CD 1114.X.53). Two years later, Oswald would deny in an FBI interview that he had taken his birth certificate. But in 1960 Hoover used the mother's claim to stake out an FBI and Security Office interest in the case:

> Since there is a possibility that an imposter is using Oswald's birth certificate, any current information the Department of State may have concerning subject will be appreciated. (CD 1114.X.53)

Reiterating the possibility of an "imposter," the Security Office (SY) asked to be kept informed "for transmittal to the FBI" (CD 1114.X.53); it renewed the request six months later, after another FBI probe, and was assured by one of the divisions handling the case (Soviet) that all future information "will be forwarded to SY for transmittal" (CD 1114.XI.19).

It was not. As the State Department's ten pre-assassination files on the Oswalds grew more and more voluminous, it became customary to route from seven to nine copies on incoming dispatches on Oswald to State's Bureau of Intelligence, and from ten to fifteen copies to the CIA—but none to the Office of Security or to the FBI, even though SY had been routinely notified of Oswald's original defection. This anomaly led briefly to two opposing official attitudes towards Oswald's citizenship status. On July 7, 1961, FBI and SY (which had no jurisdiction) told the Visa Office that Oswald "renounced U.S. citizenship" (18 H 383, 385). On October 6, the Visa Office (without telling SY) advised Immigration officials that Oswald was still a citizen (22 H 24), a decision not officially ratified by State officials until December 28.

The Office of Security, like the Senate Internal Security Subcommittee with which it collaborated, owed its existence and power to the FBI-inspired McCarran Act of 1952, an outgrowth of the Hiss case and McCarthy attack on the State Department. Even in 1959 the Office of Security, along with the FBI, suffered poor relations with other parts of the State Department, which it was charged to spy on by the McCarran Act. In 1960 the status of the Security Office within the department deteriorated still further. In part this was because of the election of a new Democratic administration. Kennedy brought in a new team of liberals to supervise all security and consular affairs and curtail the power of the Red-hunters. The new team gradually dismantled the old Office of Security and eventually, on November 8, 1963, suspended Otto Otepka, the most militant of Hoover's allies in Security. Otepka had been one of the three or four individuals checking, along with Hoover, into the anomalous Passport Office treatment of the Oswald case (26 H 45). Otepka's Senate friends, the Internal Security Subcommittee, later heard that Otepka had had a defector file, including the Oswald material, in his office safe from "long prior to November 1963,"[9] the date when the safe was forced open by members of the new Kennedy team.

Internal Divisions Over Cuba

But the troubles of Security and Otepka began even before Kennedy took office. The rise of Castro to power in 1959 had caused a right-wing "Cuba Lobby" in Congress to look for scapegoats within the State Department who had "lost Cuba," like their "China Lobby" witch hunt ten years earlier which had resulted in the McCarran Act. The Senate Internal Security Subcommittee, aided by Senator McCarran's old counsel Julien Sourwine, soon attacked two State Department employees, William A. Wieland and Roy R. Rubottom, for having opposed those intelligence officers who called Castro communist. But the attack ran into trouble when it was found to be supported not only by members of the old China Lobby but by bribes and lies from operatives serving dictator Rafael Trujillo of the Dominican Republic, who by 1960 was virtually at war with the U.S. State Department.[10] In 1961 Trujillo would be assassinated; State and CIA not only knew of the plot, but smuggled in arms by diplomatic bag to the assassins.[11]

When members of the new Kennedy team discovered that Otepka was opposing them by leaking confidential material to Sourwine, they in turn began spying on him. Otepka, too, was virtually at war with his own department, while enjoying the support of J. Edgar Hoover's top allies in Congress (like Senator Thomas Dodd and Congressman H. R. Gross).

The sharp differences in State over how to handle the Oswald file, in other words, involved at least one of the key figures in a sharp internal dissension on how to handle Fidel Castro. It was apparent from almost the day they took office that the Kennedy brothers would oppose Trujillo's lobbying activities, which were not confined to attacking Castro: in June 1960 the Eisenhower administration had been forced to deal with a major scandal involving proposed changes in the legislation for sugar import quotas which would have been favorable to the Dominican Republic.[12] The first wire tapping done by the FBI for the new Attorney General, Robert Kennedy, was in the hotel room of the Congressman suspected of involvement in the sugar lobby scandal, Harold Cooley, chairman of the House Agricultural Committee.[13]

Over the years the Trujillo lobbyists in Washington, like those of the Somoza family dictatorship in Nicaragua, had built up a network of influential contacts ranging from mafiosi and their hoodlums (e.g., Joe Zicarelli of the Bonanno family) to corrupt Congressmen and their bagmen (e.g., associates of Lyndon Johnson's Senate sidekick Bobby Baker), to the domestic political machine of the Teamsters (like the Nicaragua-Teamster lobbyist I. Irving Davidson).[14] The Somozas' mob links, according to U.S. government investigators, were cemented by kickbacks to organized crime through the banking of foreign aid loans.

Bobby Kennedy's crusade to rid the Democratic Party of this Trujillo-Somoza-underworld lobby eventually led members of the Kennedy "new team," in what many would regard as an abuse of executive power, to place a bug on Otepka's telephone. Discovery of the bug led to the hurried resignation of two members of the Kennedy "new team," but not of their boss David Belisle, an old friend and close associate of Walter Sheridan, Bobby Kennedy's top trouble-shooter in his war against organized crime.[15]

Nicaragua and CIA Divisions Over Oswald and Cuba

So far we have seen that the Oswald case, and the internal disputes it generated, had become involved in the Kennedy campaign against a corrupt coalition using anticommunism as an ideological weapon to influence the State Department. The Schweiker-Hart revelations about the CIA's handling of the Oswald case, and also of assassination plots against Castro, indicate that here, too, there were deep internal divisions over the Oswald case that related to fundamental divisions over what to do about Cuba. These are most conspicuous after the assassination: at a time when the CIA's Miami Station noted sensibly that anti-Castro Cubans were spreading rumors linking Oswald to Castro "in [an] attempt [to] provoke strong U.S. action against Cuba," [16] the CIA Station in Mexico was lending its weight to one such rumor, the so-called story of "D."

"D," as he was called in the Warren Report, was an agent in Mexico City of the Nicaraguan Secret Service, who claimed to have seen pro-Castro Cubans at the Cuban consulate speak to Oswald about assassination and pass him a large sum of money on September 18, 1963 (R 307-08, cf. SHR, p. 28). "D" 's story did not hold up for long, especially after he was told that Oswald did not arrive in Mexico City until September 27. After the U.S. government had expressed its concern about the implications of his story, "D" was reinterviewed by Mexican Internal Security police at the FBI's request, and he retracted his story on November 30. Reinterviewed again with the CIA present, "D" claimed that the Mexican police had pressured him into a false retraction. He then repeated this last statement during a polygraph test, apparently administered by the FBI, which indicated he was lying. In the words of the FBI report, "D" then "stated that he had heard of the polygraph and respected its accuracy. He added that if the polygraph indicated he was lying, then that must be so." (CD 78.5)

"D," in retrospect, sounds like a confused agent responding to different indications (from FBI and CIA) as to what he was to say. He himself admitted on November 30 that the purpose of his false story was to "help cause the U.S.A. to take action against Castro" (CD 1000 D). Yet the CIA station officer who interviewed "D" called him a "well-known Nicaraguan . Communist underground member" (rather than a member of the Nicaraguan Secret Service) and also a "quiet, very serious person who speaks with conviction" (CD 1000 A, CD 1000 B.4).

Nothing that the CIA has released so far points out (as was publicly reported at the time) that the Nicaraguan Secret Service, aided by the ruling Somoza family, was engaged in plotting with many of the CIA's Cuban protégés (notably Manuel Artime) against Fidel Castro.[17] Tad Szulc has written that the CIA was behind the Artime-Nicaraguan plan, Operation Second Naval Guerrilla, which was counting on the assassination of Castro by Rolando Cubela alias AMLASH.[18] The Church Committee has indirectly confirmed many of Szulc's claims, particularly that the CIA, using Artime as a cut-out, supplied Cubela with a high-powered rifle and silencer to assassinate Castro (*Assassination Report*, pp. 89-90). Twice, despite warnings, Somoza-Artime activities had violated President Kennedy's ban on U.S.-based guerrilla operations, and one if not both of these incidents involved the future burglars of Watergate.[19]

The Schweiker-Hart Report correctly chides the CIA for failing to inform the FBI and Warren Commission about its involvement in these and other assassination plots. How much worse was the deadpan transmission by CIA station personnel of "D" 's story to the White House, without any apparent warning about his role as a Nicaraguan agent, or Nicaragua's active involvement in anti-Castro plotting, some of which had clearly violated the Kennedy government's guidelines. In fact at least four (perhaps six) of those associated at this time with the Artime-Nicaragua plan disseminated similar stories linking Oswald (or Ruby) to Fidel Castro.[20] Not once did either the CIA or the FBI point out to other authorities the connections of these personnel to active anti-Castro plots.

This would have been bad enough even if Nicaragua could have been considered a friendly anticommunist ally. But in fact the Somoza brothers of Nicaragua were working with the remains of the Trujillo intelligence network in the Caribbean, and above all the corrupt network of influence in Washington which Attorney General Bobby Kennedy had attacked. Thus the Kennedys were said to be behind the Fulbright Committee investigation of 1963 (with covert help from the Justice Department) into the lobbying activities of I. Irving Davidson, registered lobbyist for Nicaragua and Haiti.[21]

Davidson, who according to *Life* had strong Teamster and even Mafia connections, also represented the powerful domestic interests of the Texas Murchison family, who in turn were close to both Lyndon Johnson and above all J. Edgar Hoover.[22] Davidson was the contact in a Murchison business deal which resulted in a large payoff to Johnson's Senate bagman, Bobby Baker, who in turn was involved in complex Dominican Republic hotel deals with American contacts of the late dictator Trujillo.[23]

Most important, when the FBI and CIA covered up the recurring presence of the Artime-Nicaraguan conspiracy behind a spate of false

Oswald-Castro stories, they were concealing a trail to a government whose registered agent, I. Irving Davidson, was mobilizing Teamster political influence to keep Jimmy Hoffa, perhaps Bobby Kennedy's most powerful domestic enemy, from going to jail.[24] The fact is that both the FBI and the CIA would have had problems if this trail had been exposed. The CIA in particular, although it had contributed to Trujillo's overthrow, had continued to work closely in its anti-Castro activities not only with the Somozas, but with American contacts of Trujillo and the Somozas like William Pawley, whose own business connections overlapped with those of the Teamster-Murchison-Miami Cuban network.[25] Pawley had been a key witness in the Cuba Lobby's attack on Wieland.[26]

The Oswald Skeleton in the CIA Closet

The CIA also had to worry about a string of false Oswald stories, dating back *before* the assassination to 1960, which its own officers had generated or transmitted. At the beginning these falsifications had been innocuous enough, suggesting at the worst that Lee Harvey Oswald, when in the Soviet Union, had been on some kind of intelligence mission whose cover they were protecting. This would explain the American Defectors List prepared by the CIA in November 1960 for the White House: in that list of fourteen names, the life history of one defector, "Lee Henry Oswald," had been so altered (even in a secret memo) as to make him untraceable (CD 692).

These alterations, by a CIA officer in Washington, were not a one-time accident. In December 1960 the CIA "opened" a file on "Lee Henry Oswald," in which they stored, without even the required cross-reference, all of their extensive information about Lee Harvey Oswald (and his wife Marina, whose name Prusakova was similarly misrendered as Pusakova). This may well have been a device to protect its own records, as when CIA officer Birch O'Neal (a former station chief in Guatemala, 1954) reportedly told the FBI right after the assassination that there was no CIA-generated material "in CIA file regarding Oswald" (CD 49.22). At this time Naval Intelligence, Army Intelligence, and the Dallas Police were all likewise transmitting and/or filing material about, or under the name of, *Harvey Lee* Oswald.

There was a lot of CIA-generated material about Lee *Henry* Oswald.

Beginning in October 1963 the CIA disseminated to other agencies a series of CIA messages about "a man who identified himself as Lee Oswald, [who] may be identical to Lee Henry Oswald" who had "contacted the Soviet Embassy in Mexico City" (CD 361).[27] These stories were not as innocuous as those in 1959-60, for they alleged that Oswald had spoken with Valeriy Vladimirovich Kostikov, identified in CIA files as connected with the Soviet KGB assassination department (CIA-1, cf. 17 H 812). According to the CIA, this Oswald "was described as approximately 35 years old, with an athletic build [and] a receding hairline." Lee Harvey Oswald at this time was twenty-three years old, and slender. Photos taken in Mexico City of this reported thirty-five-year-old were given by the CIA to the FBI on November 22, and one of these (the so-called Odum Exhibit, 20 H 691) was shown by Dallas FBI agent Bardwell D. Odum to Marguerite Oswald the next day (11 H 468-69).

What all this bureaucratic nonsense was about is still very obscure; what is clear (as Paul L. Hoch has shown through meticulous research) is that the CIA, and then-Deputy Director Richard Helms in particular, devoted considerable energy to obstructing a public resolution of these anomalies by the Warren Commission.[28]

Oswald and the CIA's Anti-FPCC Campaign

It is particularly intriguing to learn from the Schweiker-Hart Report that the CIA, in September 1963, was giving "consideration to countering the activities" of the pro-Castro Fair Play for Cuba Committee (FPCC) in foreign countries (p. 65); and that as a direct result of the CIA's request, the FBI "uncovered a letter Oswald had written [FPCC National Director] Ted Lee about Oswald's FPCC activities in New Orleans" (p. 66). The report scrupulously notes that "there is no reason to believe that any of this FBI or CIA activity had any direct connection with Oswald" (p. 66). But Oswald's FPCC activities have many telltale signs that they were a public relations or "psychological warfare" operation, conducted under U.S. intelligence auspices, to link the FPCC (through Oswald) to the USSR.

Oswald's much-publicized arrest at his first conspicuous FPCC leafleting was for disturbing the peace through a "fight" which never occurred (10 H 38), with Carlos Jose Bringuier, the former Press and Propaganda Secretary of the CIA-sponsored Cuban Revolutionary

Council (CRC) in New Orleans. The arrest took place in front of a store where Bringuier had once worked (10 H 37). At least some of Oswald's leaflets were stamped with the CRC's former local address when Bringuier was its officer (544 Camp Street). A local TV station (WDSU) covered Oswald's insignificant trial (10 H 39) and his second leafleting five days later. This leafleting took place in front of the old International Trade Mart in New Orleans, whose director Clay Shaw has since been identified along with Bringuier as a one-time CIA domestic contact (CIA 502.3). The FBI's witnesses to the leafleting were the public relations director for the Trade Mart (Jesse R. Core III, who later was District Attorney Jim Garrison's campaign manager), at least one other PR man, and several of their friends (CD 75.690; CD 6.414-16).

Finally, Oswald and Bringuier debated together on station WDSU, and Oswald was exposed by a third participant, Bringuier's close friend Ed Butler, as a man who had "turned in his passport" in Moscow and "applied for Soviet citizenship" (21 H 639). Butler's cited sources were Washington newspaper stories which he later explained he had obtained "through a third party in Washington." [29] This dramatic "proof" of the FPCC's Communist background was then recorded as a "truth tape" for distribution to radio stations throughout Latin America by Ed Butler's "psychological warfare" organization, the Information Council of the Americas, or INCA (CD 75.471). Oswald's self-revelation as an FPCC "Marxist" on that tape was given by Bringuier and Butler to the world on November 22, 1963 (right after Oswald's arrest); and as a result the FPCC decided to close down shortly thereafter. [29a]

It is not unreasonable to suspect U.S. government sponsorship of Butler's INCA operation. On September 12, 1963 (four days before the CIA contacted the FBI about the FPCC), Butler returned to Washington, and told a House Committee about his "truth tapes" activity through INCA, which he conceived of while serving in a special U.S. Army unit "in the quiet little town of Alexandria, Virginia." [30] (At least four of the other five speakers with Butler represented groups, like the Cuban Freedom Committee and Radio Free Europe, since identified as CIA fronts. [31]) One of Butler's prize speakers for his truth tapes was Fidel Castro's anticommunist sister, Juanita, who also served on INCA's Advisory Committee. The CIA engaged in major propaganda activities against Salvador Allende in the Chilean election of 1964, in which a prominent role was played by right-wing radio tapes featuring Juanita

Castro (though it is not yet known whether or not these were Ed Butler's INCA "truth tapes").[32]

INCA's links to both Oswald and the U.S. government were considerable. INCA's president was the famous doctor Alton Ochsner, a consultant to the U.S. Air Force "on the medical side of subversive matters"; Ochsner, a friend of the Somozas, was later identified as "the first man to uncover Oswald's pro-Communist activities"—from unexplained "first-hand impressions."[33] Ochsner also sponsored a local journal, *Latin American Report,* whose editor (William G. Gaudet) admitted a CIA connection and also was issued the Mexican travel permit immediately preceding Oswald's (CD 75.588).[34] At least three of INCA's backers and Cuban employees had previously been associated with the CIA-backed Cuban Revolutionary Council at 544 Camp Street.[35] More important, the Reily family (Eustis Reily of INCA, William Reily of the CRC Crusade) were Oswald's ostensible employers in New Orleans.[36] Another INCA charter member, William I. Monaghan, an ex-FBI agent, joined the Reily Company about the same time Oswald apparently did, and soon became the chief source of information to the FBI and Secret Service about Oswald's activities with the company (23 H 700; 26 H 763-64).[37]

INCA's and Butler's intelligence links became more apparent after 1963, when Butler added to his letterhead foreign intelligence and psy-war personnel, and himself joined such well-known CIA friends and veterans as Christopher Emmet and Edward Lansdale on the Planning Committee for the Freedom Studies Center of the American Security Council. (Although the ASC was staffed largely by ex-FBI personnel, it was revealed because of Watergate that at least one of these, Lee R. Pennington of the ASC Washington Bureau, was also on a CIA monthly retainer.[38]) By 1969 Butler and other INCA personnel were actively involved in the White House counter-demonstrations to the growing antiwar movement.[39]

There was also a private side to INCA's story, however. Much of INCA's support came from large private firms in New Orleans that were active in the Caribbean, feared expropriation there, and thus worked closely with both the CIA and corrupt local governments like Nicaragua. Perhaps the most important of these was Standard Fruit and Steamship, which made payoffs to Central American governments and later, along with Frank Sturgis and Howard Hunt, was accused of plotting the assassination of Panamanian President Omar Torrijos.[40] Standard Fruit and Steamship has also been named for its role in ensuring Mafia control of corrupt Longshoremen's union locals in the United States (one ILA local owned the building at 544 Camp Street).[41]

Standard Fruit's employees at INCA included its General Counsel Eberhard Deutsch (Jim Garrison's former law partner and political mentor); Cuban refugee activist and CRC-veteran Manuel Gil, who helped arrange the Oswald-Bringuier "debate"; and William I. Monaghan, who later resigned and joined Oswald at the William B. Reily Company. And a "Charter Member" of INCA was Standard Fruit's director Seymour Weiss, a veteran anticommunist and political heavy from the Huey Long era. Weiss was said to have run New Orleans for the National Crime Syndicate along with the more famous mafioso Carlos Marcello.[42]

CIA-Mafia Collaboration in the Caribbean

The CIA had long used the Mafia's corrupt influence in Caribbean dictatorships as an asset in its own anticommunist arsenal. Thus the chairman of a 1958 anticommunist conference in Guatemala (of a group organized for the CIA four years earlier by E. Howard Hunt) was Antonio Valladares, the law partner of the CIA-installed minister of the interior and the attorney for New Orleans mafioso Carlos Marcello; Valladares once arranged for Marcello's false birth registration in Guatemala.[43] (Present at the 1958 meeting was a New Orleans lawyer, Maurice B. Gatlin, who was also involved in other anticommunist activities at the 544 Camp Street address used by Oswald.[44]) In March 1963 Guatemala experienced the first of a series of right-wing coups which lined up new governments in support of the Somoza-Artime-Cubela project to overthrow Castro.[45] It was followed by the Dominican Republic coup of September 25, 1963, and the Honduras coup of October 2, 1963.

For some time it has been known that in 1963 Carlos Bringuier was involved in an anti-Castro Cuban exile training camp of the Christian Democratic Movement (MDC) on Lake Pontchartrain, a camp which Bringuier accused Oswald of trying to infiltrate (CD 984B.19-28; SHR, p. 12). The camp was owned by the political de la Barre family with landholdings in Guatemala; and, according to MDC chief Laureano

Batista, Somoza himself had given the green light for the training camp, whose graduates were to have been sent on to Nicaragua.[46]

The Schweiker-Hart Report now reveals that "anti-Castro exiles *and underworld figures* . . , were operating the guerrilla training camp" (p. 79). It links these operators to an unnamed Cuban exile (whom it calls "A"), an alleged life-long friend of Cubela who knew about the CIA's contacts with him to assassinate Castro (p. 78). In 1963 "A" had transported twenty-four hundred pounds of dynamite to a house near the training camp, which was raided by the FBI on July 31, 1963. The underworld was involved with this arms cache as well. One of those arrested after the raid was Sam Benton, a longtime resident in Cuba under Batista and a major figure in the sophisticated placement of fraudulent securities at mob-controlled banks, banks which once channeled casino profits from Cuba. According to Senate hearings, Benton operated in these placements with Mike McLaney, a former casino operator in Havana and a personal friend of J. Edgar Hoover; McLaney's brother William owned the house raided for dynamite by the New Orleans FBI.[47]

The Schweiker-Hart Report has assembled evidence to suggest that this Cubela–arms cache–Bringuier-Oswald connection lies at the center of the ensuing FBI-CIA cover-up (SHR, pp. 12-13, 77-79). Many critics would agree. In fact the connection was stronger, and politically more influential, than the report could properly suggest. Sam Benton, for example, was indicted in 1971 with the brother of a New York Mafia boss, and with Dinty Whiting, former Army Intelligence officer and lawyer (until disbarred in 1961) with the influential Miami firm of Salley and Roman, attorneys for the so-called Ansan group which laundered millions of dollars in Cuban money into Key Biscayne real estate deals involving the Teamsters and Richard Nixon.[48]

The principal member of the Ansan group was Jose Aleman, a former Cuban minister under President Prio; Aleman's son Jose Jr. was a close friend of Cubela (AMLASH) and financed his anti-Batista operations in the 1950s.[49] But another Ansan associate, ironically, was Batista's investment ally Anselmo Alliegro, whose Miami bank (Pan-American National) was allegedly used by Benton and McLaney for the placement of worthless securities.[50] A third associate was Agustin Batista (no relation to the dictator) whose brother Laureano headed the Cuban Christian Democratic Movement in charge of the Lake Pontchartrain training camp.[51] The Cuban in charge of the MDC training camp, Victor Paneque Batista, was Laureano Batista's personal assistant and allegedly his nephew; in Havana he had once headed up an underground for displaced casino operators and their chief of operations, the future Watergate burglar Frank Sturgis.[52]

What may have embarrassed the CIA was its own involvement in this underworld connection, for operations which (to judge from other Church Committee revelations) may have been unauthorized and even prohibited by the Kennedy White House. In 1962, when the CIA falsely notified Robert Kennedy that it had terminated its Mafia underworld contacts, he retorted angrily, "I trust that if you ever try to do business with organized crime again—with gangsters—you will let the Attorney General know." (*Assassination Report,* pp. 133-34) The CIA did not so inform him, and indeed the Church Committee found no authorization for any kind of covert operations against Castro in 1963 until June 19, or four days *after* a group of McLaney associates, including both Benton and "A," had been detained by U.S. Customs agents for attempting to bomb the Shell Refinery in Cuba (*Assassination Report,* p. 173; cf. SHR, p. 12).[52a]

Fortunately for the CIA, Frank Sturgis's friend Jack Anderson had already published a report that Mike McLaney had "sent the CIA a detailed plan for knocking out the . . . refineries . . . but instead . . . got an urgent phone call warning him not to attempt a thing under the circumstances."[53] But the public record is clear that, as part of the CIA-Artime plan, MDC leader Laureano Batista and Aleman-ally Prio were meeting Luis Somoza, along with Artime's representative Miguel de Leon (author of one of the false Oswald stories).[54] The MDC-underworld training camp, in short, was *part* of the CIA-Artime-Cubela-Somoza plan.

All this was known before. We learn for the first time from the Schweiker-Hart Report of "A" 's "involvement with anti-Castro exiles *and underworld figures* who were operating the guerrilla training camp" —underworld figures in a further apparent violation of Robert Kennedy's directive.[55] Then in 1965 "A" gave information to the FBI (and CIA) about the AMLASH (Cubela) plot, which "suggested a link between the AMLASH operation and the 1960-62 CIA plots to assassinate Castro using underworld contacts."[56]

This important quote from the Schweiker-Hart Report is based on a secret investigation by the CIA's Inspector General in 1967, which in turn was triggered by a provocative Drew Pearson–Jack Anderson column of the same year, suggesting that CIA-underworld plots against Castro might have "helped put into motion forces that indirectly" led to the John F. Kennedy assassination. A second Anderson column of 1971 on the anti-Castro plot has since been largely corroborated by the Church Committee's *Assassination Report,* which greatly strengthens the apparent links between the Castro and John F. Kennedy assassination plots.[57]

The CIA-Mafia Plot Against Castro

In 1960, while Vice-President Richard Nixon was still the White House executive officer for the CIA's Cuban operations, the CIA had indeed contacted at least three mafiosi, John Roselli of Las Vegas, Sam Giancana of Chicago, and Santo Trafficante, Jr., of Havana and Tampa, about arrangements to assassinate Castro.[58] Roselli later told Jack Anderson that "Cubans from the old Trafficante organization," allegedly working with "Cuban intelligence," were the forces in the old CIA plot to which he attributed the Kennedy assassination.

This story explains the attention paid by the CIA Inspector General and the Schweiker-Hart Report to "A" 's "link" between the CIA plot and AMLASH (Cubela), the deputy minister for Cuban intelligence. Roselli and "A," it would appear, may both have been talking about the same "links." For Trafficante in 1962 was in close touch with Cubela's former Miami bankroller, Jose Aleman, Jr.; and the lawyer for his bolita gambling interests, "Richard G. Taylor," was later said by an informant to have been involved in the fraudulent securities operations of "A" 's friend Sam Benton—operations which (like Trafficante himself) have been suspected of financing the international narcotics network.[59]

Various sources have suggested that, as late as 1962-63, Trafficante was still in some kind of contact with the island of Cuba, whether (a) with the government (the Federal Bureau of Narcotics reported in 1961 rumors that Trafficante was "an agent of Castro" and his "outlet for illegal contraband"), or alternatively (b) with anti-Castro groups who paid for their operations with narcotics, or (as I suspect) (c) with the remaining French-Corsican Mafia casino operators in Havana, whose political allegiance was too complex to be easily characterized.[60]

A senior CIA official, Scott Breckinridge, suggested to the Church Committee staff that Trafficante had in fact been reporting to Castro all the details of the proposed CIA-Mafia plot to kill him.[61] More recently press interviews with Frank Sturgis, the convicted Watergate burglar and former CIA operative, have suggested that the assassination of Castro was discussed in 1963 during a personal meeting between Fidel Castro and Jack Ruby, to negotiate a drugs-for-guns deal.[62] Right-wing sources with U.S. intelligence and police connections have been suggesting just such a Castro-drugs-Ruby plot since as early as January 1964 (20 H 746, cf. 718-19).

But Sturgis, at least, is hardly a disinterested or objective source. A former employee of the displaced casino operators who were plotting against Castro, he was a long-time associate of Cubela's and Aleman's co-plotter Eugenio Rolando Martinez, the CIA operative arrested with Sturgis in Watergate.[63] An MDC-Somoza anti-Castro mission of October 1963, from a Florida-based ship of the Somozas called the *Rex,* involved both Martinez as skipper (according to Sturgis) and very probably Sturgis himself as well. This Florida-based raid violated President Kennedy's publicly announced prohibition of Cuban exile raids "launched, manned, or equipped from U.S. territory."[64] It came only one month after Sturgis himself had been publicly warned by U.S. government officials to desist from just such activities.[65]

At present the accusations that Fidel Castro was involved in the narcotics traffic remain unproven. It is unfortunately an amply documented fact that many of the CIA's anti-Castro operatives financed their activities from the narcotics traffic through Miami.[66] It has been frequently alleged that Manuel Artime's bases in Costa Rica for Operation Second Naval Guerrilla, one of which was a ranch owned by the Somozas, had to be closed down in 1965 because they were being used for major smuggling operations, including cocaine.[67] One Cuban who transmitted a false Oswald-Cuban intelligence story from Artime's Nicaraguan coordinator Miguel de Leon (CD 770.3-6, cf. 26 H 302-03) is today reportedly serving a twenty-year sentence in the Atlanta federal penitentiary for his part in a Cuban exile–Trafficante-Mafia cocaine operation.[68]

Mafia Resentment Against the Kennedys

Like his father before him, Santo Trafficante himself has been recurrently identified as a principal in Caribbean and perhaps world narcotics operations.[69] And like his close Mafia associate Carlos Marcello in New Orleans, Trafficante has also been accused of voicing pre-assassination threats or warnings against John F. Kennedy: "Mark my words, this man Kennedy is in trouble, and he will get what is coming to him. . . . he is going to be hit."[70] But Trafficante's reported anger against Kennedy derived not from the President's Cuba policies, but much more understandably from the anti-Hoffa anti-organized crime drive of his brother, the attorney general.

Trafficante's ominous prediction, according to the *Washington Post*, was made to Cubela's old friend Jose Aleman, Jr., at a time when he was offering to obtain a loan for Aleman from the Teamsters Union. Aleman claims that he appropriately warned the FBI at the time, but that they showed no interest in the words quoted until after the assassination, when two FBI agents questioned Aleman closely about them.[71] There is, however, no indication that the FBI either pursued this lead or even transmitted it to the Warren Commission, as there is no sign that they transmitted 1964 reports of "a threat by James R. Hoffa to kill the Attorney General."[72] The FBI's handling of these reported threats should certainly be subjected to further congressional scrutiny.

The Mafia Skeleton in the CIA Closet

It is obvious that the CIA would have had strong motives in covering up a close investigation into Santo Trafficante and Sam Giancana, whether or not these two men had had anything to do with the John F. Kennedy assassination. Both in his service with the McClellan Racket Committee staff, and later in his book *The Enemy Within*, Robert Kennedy had focused on the organized crime associates of Jimmy Hoffa and his allies, specifically including both Trafficante and Sam Giancana.[73] As I suggested earlier, this campaign was not wholly disinterested. The Kennedy brothers could not hope to gain control of the Democratic Party until they had neutralized the corrupt but powerful political influence therein of men like these three (just as, conversely, it proved extremely difficult to jail Jimmy Hoffa because of Hoffa's political influence).[74]

But elements in the CIA seem to have taken steps to ensure that the anticipated Kennedy crime drive would not destroy the CIA's traditional corrupt "assets" in the Caribbean. It was in 1960, shortly after Bobby's book had named both Trafficante and Giancana, that the CIA recruited both men in its conspiracy to assassinate Castro.[75] By this act, apparently on its initiative, the CIA was extending its own mantle of immunity from the criminal law to two or more of Robert Kennedy's intended targets. At least once, and possibly twice, Giancana's lawyers (who included Robert Kennedy's enemy Edward Bennett Williams) were able to use this "CIA immunity" to save their client from prosecution by the Kennedy Justice Department.[76] Government attorneys and a star CIA witness provided similar immunity in court cases involving mafioso John Roselli, the third plotter with the CIA against Castro, and Trafficante's Havana casino partner Gabriel Mannarino, a fourth alleged plotter.[77] Trafficante himself escaped indictment altogether.

The CIA's choice of assets threatened by Kennedy does not appear to have been accidental. The decision was made by CIA Deputy Director Richard Bissell and Security Director Sheffield Edwards in August 1960, one month after John Kennedy had been chosen the Democratic candidate for president. As go-between in the Mafia contacts, the CIA selected former FBI agent Robert Maheu, then a private detective in the law firm of Edward Bennett Williams (and long-time CIA asset) who had conducted questionable investigations on behalf of Williams's most important clients, Jimmy Hoffa and the Teamsters. Maheu's activities for Williams had also come under Robert Kennedy's scrutiny in the McClellan Committee, where the hostility of Williams towards the two Kennedy brothers was if anything more apparent than that of Hoffa himself.[78]

Thus the stage had been set for CIA Security Director Sheffield Edwards to tell the FBI in 1961 "that the CIA would object to Maheu's prosecution because it might reveal sensitive information relating to the abortive Bay of Pigs invasion" (*Assassination Report*, p. 79). This was the situation that so angered Robert Kennedy when he first learned about it in 1962, at which point Edwards falsely notified him in person that the CIA's offer of payment to the Mafia casino operators "had been definitely withdrawn" (*Assassination Report*, pp. 132-33). Maheu was able to use his CIA immunity again in 1966: in that year the CIA General Counsel, after meeting with Maheu and his attorney Edward P.

Morgan (like Maheu a former FBI agent), advised Senator Edward Long
not to call Maheu to testify, as he had been "involved in CIA operations" (*Assassination Report,* p. 79). In May 1966 John Roselli,
another CIA-Mafia conspirator and client of Edward P. Morgan, also
was able to have the CIA intervene on his behalf with the FBI (*Assassination Report,* p. 85n).

The CIA-Mafia Plot as Political Blackmail

Edward P. Morgan, it is now known,[79] is the lawyer discussed in the
final and most obviously censored section of the Schweiker-Hart Report, which lacks important details recorded in the report's Chronology
and Church Committee Hearings. The Senate findings, supplemented
parenthetically by later information from Morgan and Jack Anderson,
were as follows: the lawyer (i.e., Morgan) had clients "on the fringe of
the underworld" (including John Roselli), who "faced possible prosecution" and who had been "used by the CIA in attempts against Castro"
(pp. 84-106). Through Drew Pearson (a long-time friend of both Earl
Warren and Morgan),[80] Chief Justice Warren was informed that (according to these clients) "the United States had attempted to assassinate
Fidel Castro . . . and Castro had decided to retaliate" (p. 80). The
lawyer (Morgan) told the FBI later that "his clients obtained this information 'from "feedback" furnished [to them] by sources close to
Castro,' who had been initially placed there to carry out the original
project."[81]

After the FBI had declined to reopen the assassination question,
Jack Anderson published the same "retaliation" claim in the Drew
Pearson column of March 3, 1967; the *Washington Post* finally published a follow-up version of the story on March 7. This column
prompted Lyndon Johnson to order first the FBI and later the CIA to
follow up on the allegations of the lawyer's clients.[82] The resulting CIA
Inspector General's Report of April 1967 provided, for the first time,
extensive documentary corroboration of the CIA-Mafia involvement, a
fact which has since been used to exert further pressure on the U.S.
government. That same month Jack Anderson phoned CIA Director
John McCone, who thereupon dictated an additional corroborative
memo (*Assassination Report,* p. 164n). Morgan's behavior seems far

from disinterested, if we are to believe the semi-official rumors that his client and office neighbor, and possibly even Morgan himself, enjoyed special government connections.

In this context, these complex maneuvers by Pearson, Anderson, and Morgan appear like efforts to gain additional leverage upon hostile elements in the U.S. government. This involved them with the much cruder effort by Roselli, a member of the original CIA-Mafia conspiracy, in his apparent further effort to blackmail the U.S. government by airing a disguised version of the Mafia skeleton in the CIA's closet. But in the version of Jack Anderson (a political foe of Robert Kennedy), the painful facts (CIA-Mafia collaboration without, and later against, Attorney General Kennedy's instructions) were transformed into something quite different—a personal vendetta between the Kennedys and Castro. Anderson's 1967 column exculpated the CIA, and downplayed underworld involvement as a discounted rumor: in short it said just what one might expect, in the light of his later statement that his sources were (a) the lawyer (Morgan), and (b) a contact in the CIA who had (he thought) cleared his "revelation" with CIA Director Richard Helms:

> President Johnson is sitting on a political H-bomb—an unconfirmed report that Senator Robert Kennedy (Dem.-N.Y.) may have approved an assassination plot which then possibly backfired against his late brother. ... This report may have started New Orleans' flamboyant District Attorney Jim Garrison on his investigation of the Kennedy assassination, but insiders believe he is following the wrong trails. ... The CIA hatched a plot to knock off Castro. It would have been impossible for this to reach the levels it did, say insiders, without being taken up with the younger Kennedy. Indeed, one source insists that Bobby, eager to avenge the Bay of Pigs fiasco, played a key role in the planning. ... Some insiders are convinced that Castro learned enough at least to believe that the CIA was seeking to kill him. With characteristic fury, he is reported to have cooked up a counterplot against President Kennedy.[83]

The Anderson columns somehow omitted the following relevant facts:

(a) Pearson, Anderson and the lawyer (Morgan), along with Maheu's political ally Hank Greenspun, were old political allies from their common efforts to defeat Senator Joseph McCarthy and his China Lobby cronies back in 1950-52. That campaign, like Pearson's earlier campaigns against overt fascism abroad and at home, had involved close contacts with liberal anticommunist figures close to McCarthy's targets in State and the CIA (ranging from C. D. Jackson of Radio Free Europe and John Peurifoy, ambassador during the CIA's Guatemala operation of 1954, to Averell Harriman). Pearson's defense of the administration in 1950-51 led to investigations of Pearson (and his leaks of government materials) by McCarthy's friends in the FBI.[84]

(b) These were not the first veiled allusions in the Pearson-Anderson column to the content of Morgan's story. In the months after the Kennedy assassination, Pearson had

> produced some carefully angled exclusives. The CIA, he revealed, *had assigned Cuban agents to kill Castro.* He raised the point twice that the bungled attempts might have come to the attention of Lee Harvey Oswald and focused his diffuse hostility toward a world where he could find no comfortable place. The Soviet Union turned Oswald's file over to U.S. investigators, Pearson noted in the "Merry-Go-Round," adding that the United States had never done as much for the Russians. *The purpose of the columnist-turned-diplomat was to reduce hysteria,* which might upset the delicate balance between the two countries.[85]

(c) Immediately preceding the Kennedy assassination, Pearson had been the principal personal go-between during the hesitant first steps taken by Nikita Khrushchev and John F. Kennedy towards a relaxation of tensions. After his second visit to Khrushchev in 1963 (this time with Earl Warren), Pearson had also aired in his columns the "left-CIA" hypothesis of a growing Sino-Soviet split. Pearson had found President Kennedy most attentive when he reported these matters to him; it was shortly after that Kennedy planned an approach to Peking. But Jack Anderson, a hard-line anticommunist close to some of the more belligerent CIA and foreign lobby operatives, had been displeased by these Pearson peace initiatives.[86]

(d) In 1964 Pearson, who enjoyed good personal relations with the Johnson White House, had protected Lyndon Johnson from the effects of his most threatening domestic scandal (the Bobby Baker affair), by leaking government information about a key witness, Don Reynolds, who had turned on Bobby Baker. Using government sources, Pearson revealed Reynolds to have been *inter alia* " 'an informer' for the late Senator Joe McCarthy."[87] Some of Anderson's closest anticommunist and pro-CIA lobbyist friends—notably I. Irving Davidson and Max Kampelman—were also threatened by a runaway Bobby Baker investigation.[88]

(e) In 1966-67 Pearson (if not Anderson) was using his good will at the Johnson White House to strengthen the President against primarily the hawks, but also the doves, who were now diverging publicly from his Vietnam policies. The Pearson-Anderson column of March 3, 1967, with its slanted attack at Robert Kennedy, appeared the day after Kennedy's controversial bombing-suspension proposal, and General William C. Westmoreland's public rebuttal of it, which some Washington observers correctly interpreted as a prelude to intensified bombing of North Vietnam.[89]

Anderson's "insiders" were not very credible sources for the story that Castro killed Kennedy, especially in the light of Helms's later admissions to the Church Committee that (a) Robert Kennedy never told Helms to kill Castro, and (b) Helms never told Robert Kennedy about the CIA-Mafia plots (*Assassination Report*, p. 151). In fact, as noted earlier, the CIA had falsely notified Robert Kennedy, after he was alerted by the FBI, that the plots had terminated.[90]

In view of its far from disinterested sources, this particular "Castro story" seems highly suspect; but the *hidden* story of the CIA-Mafia plot was indeed, as Anderson described it, a "political H-bomb." Its power to embarrass the government was exhibited on January 18 and 19, 1971, when Anderson repeated the story in his column, with added details from lawyer Edward P. Morgan's client, John Roselli. Senate Watergate Committee investigators learned that these two columns—which again asked, "Could the plot against Castro have backfired against President Kennedy?"—triggered a spate of memos inside the Nixon White House. These, in turn, led directly to the White House's first ill-starred contacts with Robert Bennett of the CIA-front Mullen Agency, and hence to White House dealings with Bennett's employee, the future Watergate burglar E. Howard Hunt.[91] One of these White House memos warned the President that "'Maheu's controversial activities," although not well known to the author, "might well shake loose Republican skeletons from the closet."[92] Inasmuch as Hunt himself had been an original proponent of the plot to assassinate Castro, it is quite plausible that this plot was the "Cuba thing" or "Bay of Pigs thing" Hunt knew of that President Nixon spoke of later when authorizing the illegal CIA cover-up of Watergate, since as early as 1962 it had been in-house practice to use the Bay of Pigs as a euphemism for the unmentionable CIA-Mafia assassination plot.[93]

The power of this "political H-bomb" was exhibited again in 1975, when it compelled former Warren Commission member President Gerald Ford to set up the Rockefeller Commission on CIA activities, and, because of the CIA's "assassination problem," to place former Warren Commission counsel David Belin in charge of the Rockefeller Commission's staff.[94] It is therefore important to discover why Roselli and Morgan surfaced the story in 1967.

Maheu, Hoffa and Hughes

Was it, for example, the appeal then pending before the Supreme Court (including, of course, Chief Justice Warren) of Jimmy Hoffa, a cause preoccupying not only Giancana and Trafficante but also Jack Anderson's close friend and office-mate I. Irving Davidson, the registered lobbyist for Nicaragua?[95] Hoffa's final motion to the Supreme Court on his Chattanooga conviction was filed January 27, 1967, about the time in "late January" that Pearson told Anderson's story to Earl Warren.[96] The motion was denied on February 27, and the Anderson column was published five days later, on March 3. A similar final petition for Supreme Court review of Hoffa's other conviction (in Chicago) was belatedly denied on January 11, 1971, exactly one week before the publication of Anderson's 1971 column.[97] Is it possible that publication followed the failure of the government to respond to Davidson's pressures?

Some weeks before the first column, in late 1966, Senator Russell Long, whom Sheridan names as a principal in the save-Hoffa efforts, suggested to Jim Garrison that he conduct his own investigation of the Kennedy assassination.[98] This led to Garrison's arrest of Clay Shaw on March 1, 1967, two days after the Supreme Court's denial of Hoffa on February 27. Walter Sheridan, Robert Kennedy's top trouble-shooter in the "get-Hoffa" campaign, spent most of 1967 attempting to discredit the Garrison investigation. Since then he has written that it was "intertwined" with the efforts of Teamster allies to prevent or terminate the imprisonment of Jimmy Hoffa—a campaign for which the Mafia had placed a million dollars in the hands of Garrison's friend Carlos Marcello.[99] The Garrison inquiry, according to Sheridan, became a means of applying pressure to have the government's chief anti-Hoffa witness, E. G. Partin, recant his testimony.[100]

What is most relevant about the save-Hoffa campaign is that it involved not only some of the CIA's Mafia contacts targeted by Robert Kennedy (Trafficante and Giancana) but also Anderson's friend and office-mate I. Irving Davidson, the lobbyist for Nicaragua who used Somoza money to lobby for Lyndon Johnson and even pay for Jack Anderson's hotel bill at the 1960 Democratic convention.[101] Russell Long himself is named by Anderson as a source for his column of March 7, 1967, while a Morgan-like story of retaliatory "teams" was said by a New York radio station on March 3, 1967, to be deposited in "Garrison's files."[102]

But the save-Hoffa campaign involved so many influential figures in both political parties that it was inevitably involved with other high-level political shifts at this time. One of these was the new "clean image" being given to the Teamster pension fund's investments in Las Vegas Syndicate casinos which had been investigated by Robert Kennedy. To achieve this new image, identified organized crime owners close to Hoffa were selling out to the Howard Hughes organization, while leaving their representatives in place. Robert Maheu and Edward P. Morgan played an important role in this transition, which began in March 1967.[103]

Once again, the Jack Anderson columns of 1967 and 1971 were synchronized with and related to changes in the nominal ownership of these casinos. The central figure here was Hughes's Chief of Nevada Operations Robert Maheu, the go-between in the CIA-Mafia plot. By March 15, 1967, or twelve days after Anderson's first cautious allusion to Maheu's CIA activities, Maheu had purchased his first Las Vegas casino—the Desert Inn—from Hoffa's friend Moe Dalitz (of the old Cleveland syndicate).[104] In December 1970, Maheu himself was ousted from his office by Hughes's lawyer Chester C. Davis; and shortly afterwards (through their mutual friend Hank Greenspun of the *Las Vegas Sun*) Maheu and Morgan leaked to Anderson the details in the Anderson column of January 18, 1971.[105] On March 17, 1976, two weeks before the reported death of Howard Hughes, and two weeks after further articles by Greenspun and Anderson about "documents" in their possession, the Schweiker-Hart subcommittee heard Edward P. Morgan's story, and later published it.[106]

The appearance of change in 1967 may have been more illusory than real. Moe Dalitz undoubtedly moved to his new Teamster investment at Rancho La Costa, California, and expanded that investment with a welcome infusion of hard-to-come-by cash from the Hughes purchase. But Hughes, to avoid a public appearance before the Nevada gaming commission, simply leased back the Desert Inn to its former operators.[107] John Roselli stayed on at the Desert Inn and later was given a gift-shop lease at Hughes's Frontier Hotel; two other Kennedy targets, Carl Cohen and Jack Entratter, stayed on when Hughes purchased the Sands.[108] Roselli even boasted "that he collected a large finder's fee when the Desert Inn was sold to Hughes."[109] Morgan himself collected a "finder's fee" of $150,000 on the sale of the Desert Inn, of which $25,000 went to its former PR man and minority point-holder Hank Greenspun.[110] A fourth "finder's fee" went to another minority owner, Cecil Simmons; Simmons, as it happened, was some kind of acquaintance of none other than Jack Ruby.[111]

The sale, in short, was no ordinary one. Maheu was working for Hughes, while the attorney for the other side (including Maheu's friends Dalitz and Greenspun) was Edward P. Morgan, who had represented Maheu in other matters. One of the first reports of the sale attributed it to the combined efforts of "Hank Greenspun, Ed Morgan, and Jack Anderson," adding that the three promoters "have about landed a $1 billion Federal atomic development contract for the Hughes Tool Co."[112]

Was the Howard Hughes Operation a CIA Front?

If the last report is true, government money in the form of contracts may have ultimately financed the apparent displacement of Dalitz by Hughes and Maheu in Las Vegas. Most press accounts of the deal mention the $547 million which Hughes earned in 1966 from selling his TWA stock, without mentioning his much larger income from government contracts. In fact the Hughes organization took in over $12.6 billion in government contracts between 1965 and 1976. Secret, noncompetitive CIA contracts accounted for $6 billion, while 80 percent of the remaining non-CIA contracts were also let without competition.[113]

Since this averages out to about $1 billion of non-competitive government contracts a year, it seems reasonable to state that the government and above all the CIA were ultimately financing the private intelligence activities of first Robert Maheu and after 1970 the Intertel group (International Intelligence, Inc.) which replaced Maheu at the controls of Hughes Nevada Operations (HNO).[114] For HNO did not earn money; it loaned or even gave it away liberally, much of it to men like Hank Greenspun who before 1966 had enjoyed the same kind of privileged status with the Central States Pension Fund of the Teamsters.[115] Meanwhile, in 1967 HNO and other Las Vegas casinos negotiated what the Justice Department later called a "sweetheart contract" with the local Teamsters, by paying off their "labor consultant," Sidney Korshak, named in the 1943 Roselli extortion case.[115a] It was as if the Nevada casinos, the biggest money laundry in the nation, had been taken over after 1966, when the Mafia connections were becoming obvious, by men like Robert Maheu, who handled a cash flow from the U.S. government.

Not, however, the government in the constitutional sense—that administered by the White House and under the budgetary control of Congress. Neither the White House nor Congress was powerful enough to control the secret funds and secret operations of Robert Maheu and later of Intertel: the inability of the Kennedys to keep track of Maheu's Mafia assassination plots was followed by Richard Nixon's inability to keep the Hughes-Intertel representative in Washington, Robert Bennett of the CIA-front Robert R. Mullen Company, from leaking stories to Robert Woodward which would ultimately force Nixon from office.[116]

The para-government which funded the Hughes operations was more powerful than the visible earthly operation we read about in the press. In the 1950s the Hughes operations were at the center of the "military-industrial complex" which President Eisenhower warned of on leaving public life. Pentagon officials laid the plans to make Hughes Aircraft "an unofficial laboratory for the air force":

> By 1953 Hughes Aircraft were employing 17,000 and had almost a monopoly on air force electronic systems, with a backlog of $600,000,000 in federal contracts.[117]

It was because of Pentagon pressure that Hughes divested himself of personal control over Hughes Aircraft in 1954, transferring it to the Howard Hughes Medical Institute, which is, at least on paper, controlled by his former personal secretary and chauffeur.[118]

With the development of spy-satellite technology in the late 1950s, CIA contracts have grown to surpass those of the Air Force:

"The huge contracts made Hughes Aircraft a captive company of the CIA," asserts one former Pentagon official. "Their interests are completely merged."[119]

Thus, when Hughes leased a small group of islands called Cay Sal in the southern Bahamas close to Cuba, and when these in the 1960-63 period became the base of offensive operations against Cuba, it is quite reasonable to see the hand of the CIA at work.[120]

The constitutional implications of this covert relationship have as yet been barely contemplated by any congressional committee. One obvious explanation for this lack of congressional review is the millions of dollars which the Hughes interests have channeled through foreign subsidiaries or outright cash gifts from the casino-laundries to the electoral accounts of politicians—not only of presidents like Johnson and Nixon, but also, allegedly, of congressional members of the old China-Cuba-Trijillo lobby (like Senator Eastland of the Senate Internal Security Subcommittee), and even of former Congressman Gerald R. Ford.[121] Another explanation, less conspicuous, is that the Hughes operations have also passed millions of dollars to the top public relations firms (such as Carl Byoir and Associates) and political law firms (such as Edward P. Morgan's), to protect the Hughes operation from exposure by Congress, press or courts.[122]

A federal court judge has noted how the legal forces of the Hughes interests (paid for by this Pentagon-CIA para-government) "completely outflank the government."[123] Maheu himself confirmed that the Hughes interests lobbied (with para-government money) to keep the government in the Vietnam war (in which Hughes Helicopters were consumed at a staggering but profitable rate).[124] And, to return to the revelations of the Schweiker-Hart Report, there are signs that the energy and resources of the Hughes interests have been devoted to distorting the truth about CIA-Maheu-Mafia plots, and perhaps to influencing public opinion about the John F. Kennedy assassination as well.

Robert Maheu had barely been installed in charge of the Desert Inn in March 1967 when writer James Phelan came to him with a memo (the so-called Sciambra memorandum) for xeroxing: when Phelan wrote about it two months later, he launched the interminable press controversy which ultimately discredited both Jim Garrison and the case he had tried to present of a CIA-Oswald plot.[125] Was the whole controversy—both the "case" and its downfall—*inspired* by PR men like Maheu? Thanks to the Schweiker-Hart Report, we know now that attention was deflected to Castro on March 20, 1967, five days after the Desert Inn sale with its lucrative fees (SHR, p. 106). We know also that the Phelan-Maheu relationship was not a casual but an enduring one: later Phelan would publicize both Maheu's charges against the "Mormon mafia" group at Hughes and also his friend Greenspun's defense against the IRS.[126] After Maheu was fired and Jack Anderson published his 1971 columns about Maheu and the Kennedy assassination, Anderson's enemies at the *Washington Observer* linked these two occurrences, and added, astutely:

> Bob Maheu is collaborating with journalist James Phelan on a book about Hughes. Perhaps the book will throw new light on the Hughes mystery.[127]

Maheu, Morgan, Anderson and the Fall of Nixon

Phelan and Maheu both figured in the ensuing public relations melodrama over the alleged Clifford Irving "autobiography" of Howard Hughes—a public relations melodrama which at that time was covered by more reporters than the Vietnam war.[128] One month after the melodrama the Internal Revenue Commissioner was still asking the multi-million-dollar question, "Is HH [Howard Hughes] alive?" (24 Wat 11663), suggesting that the IRS had not been satisfied by the December 1971 Carl T. Byoir-*Time-Life* production of a Howard Hughes phone interview.[128a] The subject of this Byoir-*Time-Life* production was a manuscript allegedly concocted by Irving, which we now know used a text by James Phelan.[129] Moreover, it was Phelan, then working for Greenspun, who initially told a *Time-Life* representative he thought the book was genuine; and it was Phelan who finally debunked the Irving manuscript by proving it was based on his own.[130] He did so on February 11, 1972, just one week after Greenspun's friend Wallace Turner had published extracts of the Irving manuscript relating to the 1956 Hughes-Nixon "loan," and John Mitchell and Gordon Liddy on the same day had first discussed a burglary to retrieve potential blackmail—the memos which Robert Maheu had taken from his days with the Hughes operations.[131] For Nixon was clearly vulnerable concerning the favors he and his family had received from the Hughes operations, favors which often appear to have been in reciprocation for political acts which ultimately benefited the CIA.[132]

This fateful Mitchell-Liddy meeting, whose eventual outcome was Watergate and the Nixon resignation, also represented a final rebuff to the repeated suggestions of Jack Caulfield inside the White House that the Nixon campaign steer clear of both Maheu and Intertel, and instead mount an independent security operation ("Operation Sandwedge") headed by himself.[133] On February 3, 1972, Wallace Turner had revealed that a large number of Maheu's explosive Hughes memos were now in Hank Greenspun's safe; and this seems to have triggered the Mitchell-Liddy meeting.[134] Mitchell met the next day to discuss illegal break-ins with future Watergate defendants G. Gordon Liddy, John Dean and Jeb Magruder. Magruder testified that one target for illegal entry was Hank Greenspun's office,[135] a claim corroborated by Howard Hunt's researches for Liddy at that time "concerning the Hughes' Tool problems in Las Vegas, the Maheu situation, and the Maheu-Greenspun alliance."[136]

Once again in the Nixon White House concern was probably aroused by a timely hint in a Jack Anderson column (January 24, 1972) that "we have evidence" (i.e., the Maheu memos with Anderson's friend Greenspun) about the Hughes-Maheu gift of $100,000 to Richard Nixon via Bebe Rebozo. This Hughes gift, which as much as any other single fact led to Nixon's downfall, had been explored at a 1968 meeting by Rebozo, Richard Danner, and Morgan.[137] Morgan, Maheu, and Anderson, by their successive actions, had established powerful leverage over Nixon and Rebozo. Supplemental leverage at the same pressure point was exerted in 1972-73 by Maheu's successors at the Hughes organization—Chester Davis, Intertel, and their Washington representatives at the CIA-front Mullen Company, Robert Bennett and E. Howard Hunt.[138] The pressure that finally toppled Nixon came from the Watergate Special Prosecutor and the Watergate Select Committee, and once again the Hughes connection was prominent. Two men were chiefly responsible for exposing the $100,000 contribution: of these Special Prosecutor Archibald Cox was the brother of Hughes attorney Maxwell

Cox (the sole law partner of Chester C. Davis), and the Chief Select Committee Investigator was Carmine Bellino, closely associated with Intertel President Robert Peloquin in the original Kennedy Justice Department drive to imprison Hoffa.[139]

Thus one of the most arresting revelations of the Schweiker-Hart Report is that, in 1967 as later with Nixon, a powerful Morgan-Maheu-Anderson team was able to exercise critical leverage upon a responsive White House—in both cases by alluding to what the Nixon White House called "Maheu's covert activities . . . with CIA" (21 Wat 9755). The result of this leverage in 1967 (White House orders for FBI and CIA documentation of Morgan's story and the CIA-Mafia plot) may seem at first glance to be trivial compared to the later result (the eventual downfall of President Nixon). But one must be struck by the similarities and indeed continuity of the leverage process under first Johnson and then Nixon, and the possibility that the first result (more specifically, the CIA Inspector General's Report of 1967) contributed to the second (Nixon's embarrassment about the "Bay of Pigs thing").

But what about the *substance* of Morgan's 1967 story? What did the grey alliance linking the CIA through Maheu to the Mafia have to do with either the activities of Lee Harvey Oswald or with the John F. Kennedy assassination? It will make more sense to answer these two questions separately.

The Grey Alliance and Oswald's Activities

It is not Oswald, but Oswald's patrons and protectors who can be consistently identified with the powerful lobby or lobbies working in 1963-64 for special causes such as Nicaragua abroad, Jimmy Hoffa at home, and later the Howard Hughes interests. One such center of influence was the Murchison family of Texas, recipients of major Teamster pension loans (at least one of them arranged by Nicaragua lobbyist I. Irving Davidson), investment allies of Trujillo and the Somozas, and the sources of possibly illegal kickbacks to Lyndon Johnson's sidekick Bobby Baker.[140] The Oswald family's exotic "baby-sitter" in Dallas, White Russian Baron George de Mohrenschildt, had once worked overseas for a Murchison oil company (Three States Oil and Gas, 9 H 202); he had also worked in Cuba for an oil trust uniting a Trujillo associate (Amadeo Barletta) with a representative (Jose I. de la Camara) of the

Batista Falla family behind the Lake Pontchartrain training camp.[141] He was also involved in a local White Russian anticommunist church which enjoyed a CIA subsidy;[142] and he was a personal friend of the CIA representative in Dallas, J. Walton Moore (cf. 9 H 235, CD 555.77). De Mohrenschildt himself suggested to the Warren Commission that he might have asked Moore "about Lee Oswald" (9 H 235).[143]

These pre-assassination Oswald leads to the CIA-Murchison connection are admittedly tenuous and inconclusive. The situation changes dramatically, however, when Oswald dies on November 24, 1963, and new protectors are brought in to manage the future affairs of his widow Marina, the key Warren Commission witness. Here, beneath the series of press accounts about Marina's fate, one detects the continuing influence of men associated with Bedford Wynne, who then was perhaps the Murchisons' top political fixer in Washington.[144] This influence began when the Secret Service, under strange and suspicious circumstances, arranged for Marina to be temporarily hidden from other government agencies.[145] The Secret Service chose a motel owned by the Great Southwest Corporation, a real estate investment controlled at that time by the wealthy Wynne family of Dallas (partners of the Murchisons) and by the even wealthier Rockefeller family of New York.[146] The Secret Service arranged for her to be interviewed in the presence of an organizer of de Mohrenschildt's CIA-subsidized church parish (2 H 344). The Secret Service helped arrange for the motel's manager to resign and become Marina's manager (CD 470.24).

This choice by the Secret Service (who along with CIA representative Moore were already the Wynne family's tenants in Dallas) was far from politically neutral. Murchison lawyers Bedford Wynne and Thomas Webb had just, in the November 22, 1963 issue of *Life* (p. 92A), been named as members of the "Bobby Baker set"; Wynne was already under federal investigation concerning government funds he was receiving through a Murchison family corporation, some of which ended up (via Thomas Webb) as payoffs to the law firm of Bobby Baker.[147]

Despite these facts (if not because of them) a Secret Service agent helped arrange for Marina to sign a contract making a Wynne employee, James Herbert Martin, her business manager (CD 470.24). Martin and his lawyer then arranged for a $25,000 payment to Marina, Robert Oswald, and themselves; this payment, ostensibly from Meredith Press for a book that would never be written, was actually arranged by two top officials of *Time-Life*, C. D. Jackson and Edward K. Thompson, through their Dallas representative Isaac Don Levine.[148] (As president of the CIA's Free Europe Committee in the 1950s, and as a special assistant to President Eisenhower for psychological warfare, C. D. Jackson had worked regularly on anticommunist propaganda for Eastern Europe with Isaac Don Levine of the CIA's Liberation Committee, and also Drew Pearson.[149]).

This was the period in which it quickly became clear that (as a Warren Commission counsel wrote in a memo of February 28, 1964) "Marina has repeatedly lied . . . on matters which are of vital concern."[150] There are signs that Marina was being coached as to what to say by those selected to be present at her private testimony. One of these people was former CIA employee Isaac Don Levine, who spent an intensive week with Marina just prior to her first testimony before the Warren Commission on February 3, 1964.[151]

Martin had his own contacts with men on the fringes of the underworld, including Jack Ruby.[152] Shortly after Marina's testimony, Martin was fired: he was replaced by a lawyer, William A. McKenzie, who appeared to have no connections with Martin. In fact, however, McKenzie had been until recently a law partner of Bedford Wynne, resigning from the Wynne law firm (which also represented George de Mohrenschildt, as well as Great Southwest Corporation) to become Marina's attorney. The Warren Commission failed to pursue unsolicited sworn testimony that McKenzie had improperly coached Marina on what to tell the FBI (2 H 321, cf. 336-37), even though an FBI memo corroborated that Marina had in fact said just what McKenzie was supposed to have told her to (22 H 785).[153]

There are signs that some members of the Warren Commission and its staff recognized that the shared backgrounds of Martin and McKenzie were too embarrassing politically to be investigated. McKenzie, for example, had moved from the law office of Bedford Wynne to that of Pete White, a lawyer who had once arranged for charges against Jack Ruby to be dismissed in 1954, and who admitted that he "ran into" Ruby again on November 20, 1963—two days before the assassination (CD 273.120). The FBI chronology of Ruby's pre-assassination movements contains this encounter with White (CD 360.130). In the Warren Commission's chronology (which adds such trivia as Ruby's thirty-minute treatment for baldness the same day) the encounter with White has been suppressed (25 H 321).

Worse, when Ruby's roommate George Senator was questioned about more than fifty names in the notebook of a Ruby employee, one entry—"Pete White—Atty—Fidelity—Un Life Bldg RI 1-1295" (19 H 73)—was for some reason passed over (14 H 295, cf. 14 H 34). The Warren Commission, which purported to be looking for links between Oswald and Ruby, should have been interested in this one—the appearance in a Ruby notebook of what it had already learned to be the address, phone number and office-mate of William McKenzie, Marina Oswald's attorney (16 H 768). If they had checked more closely, they would have noted that one of White's partners (Ivan Irwin, Sr.) came from the family law firm identified to the FBI by a Mafia representative (Paul R. Jones) as the conduit for pay-offs by organized crime to Dallas law enforcement officials (22 H 298).

One possible reason why the Warren Commission (four of whose seven members were from Congress) would avoid studying the Wynne-McKenzie-White relationship is the powerful political connections which the Wynne-McKenzie law firm enjoyed with both political parties. In January 1963 Bedford Wynne raised $500,000 from oil men and other special interests to pay off the 1960 Democratic campaign debt; but the Wynnes' real estate deals also involved powerful national and local Republican figures like the Rockefellers and Robert H. Stewart (a director of the Great Southwest Corporation).[154] A $453,000 real estate sale which they concluded with Pepsico in September 1964 is the apparent explanation for Richard Nixon's "law business" in Dallas for Pepsico from November 20 to 22, 1963, a visit which terminated just three hours before the assassination.[155] Richard Nixon should still be asked whether his trip to Dallas involved him with representatives of the Great Southwest Corporation, or of Wynne, Jaffe and Tinsley (the Wynne family law firm); since there are anomalies in his 1964 deposition to the FBI about this trip which exactly parallel anomalies in William McKenzie's testimony to the Warren Commission.[156] It seems legitimate to ask the question, possibly unanswerable at this stage, whether this brief trip had anything to do with the CIA "Bay of Pigs thing" which so troubled President Nixon after the Watergate break-in.[157]

One need not conclude, however, from these apparent symptoms of a high-level cover-up that the perpetrators were involved in the Kennedy assassination. On the contrary, if one doubts that Oswald was the lone assassin, but believes that his earlier travels had involved an intelligence assignment, then the perpetrators of the cover-up may have had no worse motive than the desire to protect that intelligence connection in the interests of "national security." The recurrent involvement of the Oswalds' protectors with CIA personnel and funds certainly suggests the presence of such a motive for their post-assassination behavior.

The disclosures of Watergate make it even more clear that the Wynne-Murchison empire (which profited both politically and financially from its Teamster connections) was also tied in with Maheu's ongoing activities for the Howard Hughes organization—activities which, according to recent accounts, had involved the CIA and its anti-Castro activities over a number of years.[158] Maheu's trips to Washington for the Hughes organization (like those of his associate and successor, Nixon-Rebozo-Smathers contact Richard C. Danner) led to recurring meetings not only with the inevitable Edward P. Morgan, but also with Thomas Webb, the Murchison attorney who along with Bedford Wynne had been named in the payment of kickbacks to Bobby Baker (20 Wat 9614-17). Richard Danner, in the years 1968 to 1973, saw even more of the key figures in the old Trujillo-Somoza-Murchison-Bobby Baker lobby: Trujillo's friend George Smathers, I. Irving Davidson (who in 1968 again attended the Republican Convention with Jack Anderson) and Clint Murchison, Jr.[159]

Thus the Schweiker-Hart revelations about the role played by Edward P. Morgan supply a link between Maheu's pre-assassination activities against Castro and the Wynne operation's post-assassination management of Marina Oswald, via a high-level Washington connection (Murchison-Wynne) still active in the era of Watergate.

The Schweiker-Hart Revelations and Jack Ruby

So much for the connection of Maheu's activities to the Oswalds' protectors—a connection which, though politically significant and highly relevant to the assassination cover-up, is also complex, murky, difficult to understand. If the Schweiker-Hart Committee had been allowed by its mandate to look at the connection of Maheu's activities to Jack

Ruby, they would have come up with a picture not only more suggestive but also relatively clear.

It would fill a whole chapter to list the organized crime–Teamster
connections of Jack Ruby in Chicago and elsewhere that were known
to the Warren Commission and their staff, yet suppressed from the
Warren Report. Take for example Ruby's service with Chicago Local
20467 of the Scrap Iron and Junk Handlers Union at the time it was
taken over by Jimmy Hoffa's top underworld ally Paul Dorfman, following a murder which Robert Kennedy had pinpointed as central to
the forging of the Hoffa-Dorfman-Pension Fund-syndicate alliance.[160]
Even though the Warren Commission had received from the FBI an
AFL-CIO report that the local was "largely a shake-down operation"
when Ruby worked for it (22 H 433)—an estimate corroborated by
press accounts of the union's criminal associates[161]—the Warren Report
ignored this:

> there is no evidence that Ruby's union activities were connected
> with Chicago's criminal element. Several long-time members of the
> union reported that it had a good reputation when Ruby was affili-
> ated with it and employers who have negotiated with it have given
> no indication that it had criminal connections (R 788).

In fact, the "several long-time members" were three survivors from
the shake-down era (22 H 436), two of whom gave as good a report to
the local under Ruby's old friend Dorfman as under Ruby. Of the three
employer witnesses, two grew up with Ruby and Paul Dorfman. The
third, Ted Shulman, had been questioned closely by McClellan Committee counsel Robert Kennedy about his "collusive deals" with Dorfman, for whom he had once been a character witness.[162] Shulman's
repeated evasions and use of the Fifth Amendment before that committee are not mentioned in the FBI memo which records from
Shulman that his old friend Jack Ruby "had no connections with the
organized criminal or hoodlum element" (22 H 320); nor did they deter
the Warren Commission from citing Shulman's misleading statement
that "Ruby might have been forced out of the union by a criminal
group" (R 788).

Ruby and Dorfman, who had known each other for a decade before
the union killing (22 H 382), qualified as organizers because of their
training as fighters: Local 20467 actually used the address of Ruby's

gym, Postl's, a notorious mob hangout,[163] before moving to that of the mob-organized Roosevelt Finance Company. Ruby had begun as a member of the Dave Miller gang (22 H 425). The Warren Commission characterizes this gang as a "spur of the moment" group of anti-Nazis (R 789), even though it knew that Miller, a former boxing referee, was the local gambling boss.[164]

The Kefauver Committee had heard Dave Miller's restaurant mentioned in connection with the recruitment of young toughs for the Hearsts in their newspaper wars, and for the related sales of racing scratch sheets by Hearst's circulation managers—Moe Annenberg and his successor James Ragen.[165] Ruby himself, along with other members of the Dave Miller gang, engaged in both these activities.[166] His friend Benny Barrish, who went west with him in the 1930s to sell Hearst papers in San Francisco, has recently been named in a questionable lease of a city golf course to an East Coast Mafia figure.[167]

The Annenberg-Ragen scratch sheet operation, which in the mid-thirties developed into the Nationwide Racing Wire Service for book-makers, has frequently been described as the key to local law enforcement corruption and political influence throughout the country. The murder of James Ragen in 1946 (for which two of Ruby's pugilist friends, Dave Yaras and Lenny Patrick, were indicted but never prosecuted[168]) consolidated this system of corruption and influence even more tightly in the hands of the national crime syndicate, particularly Sam Giancana's friend Tony Accardo:

> To attribute half the gang killings and mob violence of the forties and fifties to battles over control of this gambling empire would be a very conservative speculation. Whoever controlled the wire service "drops" in a town became master of gambling activities there. And more often than not he also controlled—the word is responsibly chosen, controlled—the community's local law enforcement agencies. . . . once you have got the patrolman—his lieutenant and his captain and the Chief—taking bribes from your organization for "protection" of a harmless little gambling enterprise, *you have got them for all purposes.*[169]

Among those rumored to have profited from the wire-service take-over was Chicago financier Henry Crown, whose leading political ally Jake Arvey used Lenny Patrick and other Ruby associates as musclemen in his and Ruby's homeland, Chicago's once-Jewish 24th Ward.[170] Much later, when Attorney General Robert Kennedy sent eighty-six investigators to Las Vegas (where by then the alleged *capo mafioso* was the CIA's contact John Roselli) one of the four announced reasons for their trip was to see "whether a race wire service is being operated there for the benefit of bookmakers through the nation."[171]

Back in the 1930s Roselli had risen to gangland prominence by muscling for the Annenberg-Ragen wire service at the Santa Anita race track near Los Angeles, where Jack Ruby sold a handicapper's tip sheet in 1933.[172] (It was at Santa Anita that, thirty years later, a young horse-tender called Sirhan Sirhan was introduced by a fellow groom to the study of the occult.[173]) Roselli was convicted in 1944 with seven other top members of the Chicago mob for labor extortion in Hollywood, through a union (IATSE) whose organizers included Ruby's brother-in-law (20 H 18). The political influence of the Chicago mob was amply illustrated in August 1947, when Roselli and four other top Chicago mobsters were unexpectedly paroled. A congressional investigation of that scandal named several of Ruby's Democratic contacts, including the Chicago mob representatives who had come south to Dallas for the Chicago wire service following Ragen's murder in 1946.[174]

One of these men, Paul Roland Jones, was particularly close to Ruby, who like Jones moved from Chicago to Dallas in 1946.[175] In 1947, when Customs agents arrested Jones for smuggling forty-eight pounds of opium into the country, Ruby was interrogated but let off (R 792). Government files are contradictory, however, as to why Ruby was not prosecuted. One account records an eyewitness account that when Ruby and his brother were propositioned in Chicago by Jones "concerning narcotics," they "refused to have any part of it" (23 H 206). But Ruby himself, when questioned in 1947, simply told the Federal Bureau of Narcotics that he had never spoken to Jones in Chicago at all, and that he was in Dallas on the day of the alleged encounter (23 H 203; cf. 24 H 516). Jones himself, like the first witness, spoke of meeting Ruby in Chicago—and gave Ruby's Chicago address (22 H 300, 478; cf. 23 H 303). The FBN's failure to pursue this obvious conflict of testimony strengthens the hypothesis that Ruby enjoyed protection as a government informant, and may even have been the underworld source who first alerted the government to the smuggling deal.[176]

A chief witness for the 1946 move of the Chicago mob into Dallas is George Butler, a Dallas policeman whom Jones contacted and who reported in 1963 he had "known Jack Ruby for years."[177] According to Butler, Jones claimed his group was behind the Ragen killing and would offer the incoming Dallas sheriff 50 percent of the take on the local wire service while organizing the Teamsters.[178] Jones also had gambling contacts in Cuba and represented the beer and whiskey interests of Al Capone's cousins, the Fischetti brothers, who in 1947 flew to Cuba with Frank Sinatra to see Lucky Luciano.[179]

Ruby also developed a business interest in Cuba, following that of Jake Arvey, whose son spent the evening of Castro's take-over with Lansky's casino representative Charles "the Babe" Barron in Havana.[180] Ruby himself visited Havana in 1959, at the expense of his gambler-killer friend Lewis McWillie, a former Dallas gangster who graduated to working for the Chicago mob.[181] In 1959 McWillie was manager of the Tropicana Casino in Havana (23 H 170); at that time the Tropicana was owned by Norman Rothman of Chicago, a former casino manager under Havana Mafia overseer Santo Trafficante, and a man who himself was allegedly approached by the CIA in connection with eliminating Castro.[182] Prior to this time Rothman had smuggled arms to Cuba with Trafficante's allies the Mannarinos, as had several Teamster underworld associates, and (according to many unrelated sources) as had Jack Ruby himself.

McWillie knew at least one and probably two of the principals in the CIA-Maheu-Mafia assassination plot. According to a report to the FBI, McWillie was a personal associate of Trafficante and other top syndicate leaders in Havana, including Meyer Lansky and his lieutenant Dino Cellini.[183] In 1960 McWillie was a pit boss at the Capri in Havana, whose most prominent Mafia owner, Trafficante associate Charles "the Blade" Tourine, had a mistress who reportedly tried with Frank Sturgis alias Fiorini to slip some fatal CIA poison to Castro.[184] After leaving Cuba, McWillie worked at the Cal-Neva Lodge in Nevada, where Frank Sinatra was an official point-holder and a hidden owner was Sam Giancana.[185] The disclosure in September 1963 that Giancana had frequented the Cal-Neva with Sinatra may explain why the FBI, two days before the assassination, was inquiring about McWillie's employment there.[186]

In the late 1950s the top Chicago mob representative named by Robert Kennedy as involved in Trafficante's Havana gambling operations was none other than Ruby's old friend Dave Yaras, whom Kennedy saw as behind the killing of James Ragen.[187] Although Yaras denied having seen Ruby in fourteen years (22 H 372), the Warren Commission received reports linking Ruby to a nationwide betting network of which Yaras was a part;[188] and in 1966 Ruby's close friend Lou Kopple was arrested for running a betting center for Dave Yaras and Lennie Patrick in Chicago.[189] Some members of this ring, notably Gil Beckley, were linked to the anti-Castro operations and securities operations of Mike McLaney and Sam Benton, the principals in the Lake Pontchartrain arms cache.[190] The betting ring was headquartered in Caesar's Palace in Las Vegas, a casino built with Teamster loans, and allegedly owned in part by Sam Giancana, but run by a group of Dorfman associates who allegedly have been since protected from exposure by Hank Greenspun.[191]

The Warren Commission, if it had been apprised of the CIA-Mafia plots, might have looked closely to see if they extended to Trafficante's Chicago associate Yaras. It did learn, for example, that Ruby in November 1963 twice phoned Teamster hoodlum Barney Baker, who with Yaras had helped organize Teamster Local 320 in Miami, and who on the eve of the Kennedy assassination had phoned Dave Yaras in Miami.[192]

Through McWillie, if not Yaras, Ruby undeniably had access to the Havana gambling underworld recruited by the CIA through Maheu to assassinate Castro. But it would be wrong to equate Ruby with McWillie or Yaras as a simple representative of the underworld. His status in Dallas was more complex, and apparently much more influential. Ruby, for example, enjoyed excellent relations with the Special Services Bureau (including the Vice and Narcotics Squads) of the Dallas Police, many of whom worked after hours for pay in his nightclub the Carousel.[193] For years Ruby had been a police informant for members of the Narcotics Squad.[194] At the time of his travel to Cuba in 1959 he was also a PCI (Potential Criminal Informant) for the FBI, who interviewed him eight times over a period of seven months.[195] After the assassination one SSB detective falsely denied to the FBI the well-established business relationship between Ruby and two former associates of McWillie in the Southland Hotel gang of Bennie Binion (James Robert Todd and Joe Bonds, 22 H 295, cf. 23 H 374).

Ruby's status as an informant is quite consistent with the numerous reports that Ruby was "the pay-off man for the Dallas Police Department" (CD 4.529) and "had the 'fix' with the county authorities" (23 H 372). As far back as 1956 the FBI had heard from a federal narcotics informant of a large international narcotics operation, where one participant "got the okay to operate through Jack Ruby of Dallas" (23 H 369). It would have been physically easy for the Warren Commission to locate and interview this informant, who was arrested by the Chicago police on April 27, 1964, just twenty days after the Warren Commission was sent this report.[196] Politically, of course, it would have been most difficult and dangerous, threatening other disclosures as momentous as that of the assassination itself. The commission decided that it had "found no evidence of any suspicious relationship between Ruby and any police officer" (R 224).

Ruby had status, moreover, with the local political establishment in Dallas as well as with the Dallas police. One of Ruby's self-professed "close personal friends" and character witnesses for his liquor license was Hal Collins (22 H 928), brother-in-law of prominent local attorney Robert L. Clark, the brother and uncle respectively of U.S. Attorneys General Tom and Ramsey Clark (CD 4.370). After the murder of Oswald, Collins sent Ruby a "congratulatory" telegram (CD 104.253), and told the FBI that when he "was in Dallas he would see Ruby 'weekly or monthly'" (CD 4.371). Republicans had once accused Robert L. Clark and his law partner Maury Hughes of being retained by the racing-wire people to arrange the controversial parole in 1947 of John Roselli and other top mobsters.[197] Robert Clark was also reported to have been the "go-between" on all high-level political fixes, and to have personally secured the taxi monopoly in Dallas for Ruby's landlord Houston Nichols (who later sold out to, and then worked for, Clint Murchison).[198]

It is probably irrelevant that Robert Clark also served as general counsel for an airline originally organized in part by Houston syndicate pay-off connection Jack Harold Halfen, who channeled money from the Dallas-Chicago mob's slot machines in Houston to Texas politicians as high (as he claimed) as Lyndon Johnson.[199] But Halfen also "smuggled guns and surplus American bombers to Fidel Castro," in a deal which apparently involved Carlos Prio Socarras and his Texas associate, Ruby's Cuban business contact, Robert R. McKeown.[199a]

Ruby also knew at least one member (E. E. Fogelson, 23 H 346), and probably others (e.g., Billie Byars, 23 H 363), of the influential

Murchison-Wynne set of Texas gambling millionaires, the so-called "Del Charro set," who among other activities bankrolled the Gettysburg farm of President Eisenhower and paid for the annual Del Mar racetrack holidays of their good friend J. Edgar Hoover.[200] Ruby alluded circumspectly to this high-level connection in one of the most mysterious and garbled sections of his testimony before the Warren Commission, when he alluded to some Cuban gambling business linking himself to an "attorney in Dallas" called Alfred McLane (transcribed in the Warren Commission Hearings as "Mark Lane," "Lane," and "McClain" [5 H 205]). Justice Warren recognized the allusion—"Alfred was killed in a taxi in New York" (5 H 206). This was apparently the late Alfred E. McLane, who had represented the oil-gas interests of the Murchisons, Wofford Cain of the Del Charro set, and Lyndon Johnson's business representative Franklin Denius.

With political connections as high as these, one can understand why the Warren Commission declined to investigate Ruby's series of nationwide phone calls and visits in late 1963 to Teamster connections such as his Cuban host Lewis McWillie (14 H 459), convicted hoodlum Barney Baker (who once was arrested with Averell Harriman's private phone number in his pocket)[201] (25 H 244), Dorfman sidekick Irwin Weiner (25 H 246), Joseph Glaser (Sidney Korshak's top man in the Associated Booking Corporation and American Guild of Variety Artists),[202] and Teamsters Southern Conference Chief Murray W. "Dusty" Miller (later a golfing partner of President Richard Nixon and a leading candidate to succeed Teamster president Frank Fitzsimmons).[203]

The FBI heard from some of these parties that the calls related to "AGVA business": it failed to point out that Teamster-linked American Guild of Variety Artists had been investigated by a Senate Committee for its domination by associates of Sam Giancana in the Chicago Syndicate.[204] This unrecorded detail adds considerable interest to the nationwide change in AGVA's leadership between November 19 and 21, 1963—just before the assassination—and to the strange message ("Tell Jack not to send the letter today, it would be awkward in Chicago") sent from Chicago to the Dallas AGVA office on November 23, 1963—one day before Ruby shot Oswald.[205]

The Warren Commission never dealt with—and may never have received—a Justice Department internal memorandum of November 26, 1963, "indicating a connection between Rubenstein [i.e., Ruby] and

Frank Chavez and Tony Provenzano." Both these Teamster hoodlums had been indicted by Robert Kennedy: it was Chavez who threatened to kill Robert Kennedy in March 1967, and Provenzano has figured since 1975 as a prime suspect in the disappearance of Jimmy Hoffa.[206] Nor did it investigate Ruby's connections to radio-owner Gordon McLendon, whom Ruby named as one of his six "closest friends" in Dallas (20 H 39); Walter Sheridan claims that in 1971 McLendon's brother-in-law Lester May (another Ruby associate), in conjuction with Marcello sidekick D'Alton Smith, was dropping the names of McLendon and of Clint Murchison, Jr., as powerful friends of Hoffa who would help the witness Partin if he changed his testimony.[207] In 1963 Ruby had phoned D'Alton Smith's brother-in-law (Nofio Pecora), who ran narcotics and call-girl operations for Carlos Marcello;[208] and in 1970 Smith was indicted with Ruby's old friend Maurice "Frenchy" Medlevine (another veteran of the Dave Miller gang) as part of an alleged securities fraud network that included such other members of our story as Gil Beckley, Carlos Marcello, Charles Tourine, Mike McLaney, and Sam Benton, who was arrested for his part in the McLaney arms cache at Lake Pontchartrain.[209]

Parapolitics: The Dark Quadrant

The Ruby story, in other words, is not merely relevant to the revelations in the Schweiker-Hart Report: it supplies the clue as to how the various parts of that intrigue can be seen as one. But the Ruby story, because of its high-level political implications, also indicates how difficult it will prove for any congressional committee to take up the work left unfinished by Senators Schweiker and Hart. It indicates a story not of a single assassination but of an ongoing intrigue reaching through Watergate to the politics of the present day. This is the dilemma faced by those who seek the truth in this sordid story. The truth is so relevant, so important, that its very revelation is tantamount to a restructuring of our political process.

What the truth of that intrigue could be lies beyond the scope of this essay. Elsewhere I have argued that the traumatic domestic events of recent U.S. politics have arisen from conflicts fired by the changing role of the U.S. government in the service of increasingly powerful multinational banks and corporations. President Kennedy, in the last weeks of his administration, was actively exploring how to achieve detente with the Soviet Union: his initiatives envisaged a possible normalization of relations with Cuba and withdrawal of most U.S. troops from Vietnam. Only two days after his assassination, an emergency reformulation of U.S. Vietnam policy annulled Kennedy's withdrawal plans, made (as Kennedy had declined to do) a new commitment to the Saigon government, and set in motion planning for the covert operations which led to the Tonkin Gulf incidents eight months later.[210]

International events might also cast some light on the mysterious leverage exerted in 1967 and 1971 by allusions to the CIA-Maheu-Mafia plot and the Kennedy assassination. 1967 was the year of the Six Day War and of growing sentiment within parts of the U.S. establishment that the United States was overcommitted in Vietnam: even the CIA, which had helped get U.S. troops into Southeast Asia, was beginning to exert pressure on the military and the White House to get them out.[211] The paralysis of the Nixon administration throughout Watergate was accompanied by an eight-fold increase in the posted prices of world oil, which quadrupled in the last nine months of 1973 alone. This economic revolution came to its climax with the Yom Kippur War of October 1973, but President Nixon and Treasury Secretary John Connally had been accustoming the American people to the rhetoric of an "energy crisis" for the preceding two and one half years.[212] Cynics have attributed this revolution to spectacular crisis management by the same major multinational oil companies which in 1963 lobbied successfully for U.S. intervention in Vietnam, aided by the millions of dollars which they and the domestic petroleum producers passed in this period to the country's largest law firms, public relations firms, and private intelligence agencies.[213]

Thus, the split in the country at this time was real, leading to predictable paranoia, conspiracy, cover-up, and manipulative leakage on all sides. Was Jack Anderson, perhaps the leading exposer of oil lobbyists in Washington like Bedford Wynne, leaking driblets about the CIA-Mafia plot in a studied effort to counter or divert that lobby's influence? This essay cannot answer that question.

I have, however, tried to show that the invisible hands of lawyers, public relations men, and intelligence agencies, with their grey alliances to organized crime, can be discerned through the whole span of events linking Dallas to Watergate. Even when they compete, these largely covert networks, better known to each other than to the public, share a common milieu, in which fame is often a sign of declining influence.[214] The last decade has seen a significant increase in multinational corporate power, particularly in the oil industry; we must remember that the private legal and intelligence resources of these corporations can outweigh even those of the federal U.S. government.[215]

The recent rapid growth of private intelligence networks like Intertel, which (following the lead of its predecessor, Robert Maheu Associates) derived much of its income from these big oil companies, has encouraged the proliferation of what I have elsewhere called parapolitics, the conduct of affairs by veiled procedures in which accountability is consciously diminished.[216] Assassinations, cover-ups, political blackmail, public relations image-making, are all examples of parapolitics; they all represent deviations from the model of constitutional government in which public affairs are handled by public debate and rational analysis. The cumulative effect of this government by hidden process can be to demoralize the average citizen, who may simply accept that the world, and even the universe, will be dominated by occult and capricious powers. It is understandable that goodness, once associated with citizenship, is now sought by many in meditation, the I Ching, and granola.

For to us who are spectators, the events of Dallas and of Watergate have appeared like meteors in a night sky, suddenly and without warning. Not even the events themselves have been always discernible, only the trail they leave behind in our sometimes cloudy media. It is not easy from the ground to pick out the true shape of a meteor. Nevertheless, as they become more frequent, one can begin to discern in what quadrant of the sky they find their origin.

I have suggested for the events in this essay not a single conspiratorial source but a collective origin in one such quadrant—the dark quadrant of parapolitics where CIA, private intelligence, and Mafia operations overlap. The longer we ignore this area the more powerful it will surely become, as our dearly won rights under national constitutions are increasingly overshadowed by new multinational realities, in a global system where freedom and democracy are rare.

But, to return to our astronomical figure, we should not be terrified by meteors, even if the night skies remind us of our human frailty and ignorance. For to scientists meteors are no longer symbols of mystery or portents of disaster: they are needed clues to the nature of the physical universe. And as Socrates remarked so long ago, if we can find reasons behind the phenomena of the skies, we should look for no less in the affairs of men.

Notes

1. U.S., Cong., Senate, Select Committee to Study Governmental Operations with Respect to Intelligence Activities, Final Report, Book Five, *The Investigation of the Assassination of President John F. Kennedy: Performance of the Intelligence Agencies,* 94th Cong., 2nd Sess., Senate Report No. 94-755 (Washington: Government Printing Office, 1976), p. 2. Cited hereafter as Schweiker-Hart Report, or SHR.

2. *Washington Post,* June 24, 1976, A1.

3. Warren Commission, Executive Session Transcript, June 6, 1964; cited by Tad Szulc, *New Republic,* September 27, 1975, p. 10.

4. SHR, p. 39; Executive Session Transcript, January 27, 1974, p. 171, reproduced in Harold Weisberg, *Whitewash IV* (Frederick, Md.: privately published, 1974), p. 80, and by Paul L. Hoch in Peter Dale Scott, Paul L. Hoch, and Russell Stetler, eds., *The Assassinations: Dallas and Beyond* (New York: Random House, 1976), p. 138.

5. Harry and Bonaro Overstreet, *The FBI in Our Open Society* (New York: Norton, 1969), p. 274.

6. U.S., National Archives, Warren Commission Document (cited hereafter as CD) 1114.X.53.

7. U.S., Warren Commission, *Hearings Before the President's Commission on the Assassination of President Kennedy* (Washington: Government Printing Office, 1964), I, 429. Cited hereafter as H.

8. U.S., Warren Commission, *Report of the President's Commission on the Assassination of President John F. Kennedy* (Washington: Government Printing Office, 1964), p. 751. Cited hereafter as R.

9. U.S., Cong., Senate, Committee on the Judiciary, *State Department Security—1963-65* (Part XV—The Otepka Case XIII), *Hearings,* 88th Cong., 2nd Sess. (Washington: Government Printing Office, 1964), p. 1236. Cited hereafter as Otepka Hearings.

10. *Washington Post,* December 27, 1960.

11. U.S., Cong., Senate, Select Committee to Study Governmental Operations with Respect to Intelligence Activities, *Alleged Assassination Plots Involving Foreign Leaders,* Interim Report, 94th Cong., 1st Sess., Senate Report No. 94-465 (Washington: Government Printing Office, 1975), p. 199. Cited hereafter as Assassination Report.

12. Tad Szulc and Karl E. Meyer, *The Cuban Invasion* (New York: Bal-

lantine, 1962), p. 62; Drew Pearson and Jack Anderson, *The Case Against Congress* (New York: Pocket Books, 1969), pp. 421-22.

13. U.S., Cong., Senate, Select Committee to Study Governmental Operations with Respect to Intelligence Activities, Final Report, Book Two, *Intelligence Activities and the Rights of Americans*, 94th Cong., 2nd Sess., Senate Report No. 94-755 (Washington: Government Printing Office, 1976), p. 61. Cited hereafter as Church Report.

14. Arturo R. Espaillat, *Trujillo: The Last Caesar* (Chicago: Henry Regnery, 1963), pp. 180-83 (Trujillo's Washington lobby); *Life*, September 1, 1967, p. 101 (Trujillo-Zicarelli); Walter Sheridan, *The Fall and Rise of Jimmy Hoffa* (New York: Saturday Review Press, 1972), pp. 111-12 (Trujillo-Teamsters); U.S., Cong., Senate, Committee on Foreign Relations, *Activities of Nondiplomatic Representatives of Foreign Principals in the United States, Hearings*, 88th Cong., 1st Sess. (Washington: Government Printing Office, 1963), pp. 1587, 1626, hereafter cited as Foreign Lobbyist Hearings (Somoza-Irving Davidson-Teamsters).

15. U.S., Cong., Senate, Committee on the Judiciary, *State Department Security, Hearings*, 88th Cong., 1st Sess. (Washington: Government Printing Office, 1963), pp. 1-108; Sheridan, p. 450.

16. CIA Documents on John F. Kennedy Assassination, declassified 1976 (hereafter cited as CIA-), Item 27, Cable from Miami Station to DCI, 24 November 1963.

17. *Miami Herald*, July 21, 1963; *Hispanic American Report* XVI (1963), pp. 674, 761, 858; cf. Peter Dale Scott, "The Death of Kennedy and the Vietnam War," in Sid Blumenthal and Harvey Yazijian, eds., *Government by Gunplay* (New York: New American Library, 1976), p. 164.

18. Tad Szulc, *Compulsive Spy: The Strange Career of E. Howard Hunt* (New York: Viking, 1974), pp. 96-97. Szulc suggests that one of the CIA's contacts with Cubela in Madrid was E. Howard Hunt.

19. Scott, "The Death of Kennedy," pp. 164-65, 185.

20. The most relevant is a story about Cuban intelligence escape plans for Oswald with Quintin Pino [Machado], who "had been sent by Castro to Nicaragua as of 1959 to organize anti-government guerrillas there" (CD 770.6). This story originated with Sixto Mesa, administrator of Artime's MRR, and Miguel de Leon, who in 1963 was representing Artime's MRR in the Nicaraguan and Costa Rican plan to invade Cuba (CD 770.8-9, *Hispanic American Report*, August 1963, p. 761). The story was transmitted by a Cuban journalist in Florida called Fernando Penabaz, described (after his transmission of another Oswald story) as "a holder of important government posts in Costa Rica and Nicaragua" (26 H 302). For interlocking Oswald stories from other MRR and related sources, cf. 26 H 414-15, etc.

21. Foreign Lobbyist Hearings, p. 1525.

22. *Life*, May 2, 1969, p. 31 (Teamster-Mafia clients); Ralph and Estelle James, *Hoffa and the Teamsters* (Princeton, N.J.: Van Nostrand, 1965), pp. 275-77 (Davidson-Murchisons); William Turner, *Hoover's FBI: The Man and the Myth* (Los Angeles: Sherbourne Press, 1970), p. 81 (Davidson-Murchison-Hoover); San-

ford J. Ungar, *FBI: An Uncensored Look Behind the Walls* (Boston: Atlantic-Little, Brown, 1976), pp. 271-72 (Murchison-Hoover).

23. Ed Reid, *The Grim Reapers* (New York: Bantam, 1970), pp. 141-42; cf. *New York Times,* September 28, 1963, p. 8 (Baker-Murchison-Davidson); U.S., Cong., Senate, Committee on Rules, *Financial or Business Interests of Officers or Employees of the Senate, Hearings,* 88th Cong., 2nd Sess. (Washington: Government Printing Office, 1964), hereafter cited as Bobby Baker Hearings, pp. 1008-1010; Reid, p. 200 (Baker-Jack Cooper-Rafael Trujillo, Jr.).

24. Sheridan, esp. pp. 155-56.

25. *Miami Herald,* April 18, 1971: "Pawley worked closely with Allen Dulles and the CIA in recruiting young Cubans from the anti-Castro refugees arriving in Miami [for the Bay of Pigs]"; cf. E. Howard Hunt, *Give Us This Day* (New Rochelle, N.Y.: Arlington House, 1973), pp. 28, 40, 43. Richard Nixon cited Pawley, J. Edgar Hoover, and two U.S. ambassadors to Cuba as the four who supported his "minority" advocacy in 1959 of "a stronger policy . . . against Castro": Richard M. Nixon, *Six Crises,* (New York: Pocket Books, 1962), p. 379.

26. U.S., Cong., Senate, Committee on the Judiciary, *Communist Threat to the United States Through the Caribbean,* 86th Cong., 2nd Sess. (Washington: Government Printing Office, 1960), pp. 739-61.

27. Bernard Fensterwald and George O'Toole, "The CIA and the Man Who Was Not Oswald," *New York Review of Books,* April 3, 1975, p. 24; reprinted in Scott, Hoch, and Stetler, p. 451.

28. Paul L. Hoch, "CIA Activities and the Warren Commission Investigation," in Scott, Hoch, and Stetler, pp. 468-69, 480.

29. *New Orleans Times-Picayune,* November 23, 1963, p. 8; cf. R 410, 10 H 42, 11 H 168. Ed Butler is known to have been in touch at some point with the staff of Otepka's friends, the Senate Internal Security Subcommittee (CD 351). At this point, Oswald had never been mentioned in any of the committee's published hearings, suggesting that Otepka (whose interest we have already noted) may have brought Oswald to the committee's attention.

29a. "The committee, founded in 1960, had started to disintegrate before the assassination; after the murder final plans were made for liquidation" (*Hispanic American Report,* December 1963, p. 1154).

30. U.S., Cong., House, Committee on Foreign Affairs, *Winning the Cold War: The U.S. Ideological Offensive, Hearings,* 88th Cong., 1st Sess. (Washington: Government Printing Office, 1963), pp. 576-79.

31. The Cuban Freedom Committee was set up for the CIA by the Robert R. Mullen Agency, whose future employee E. Howard Hunt played such a prominent role in Watergate.

32. *Victory* (New Orleans: INCA), March 3, 1965 (INCA-Juanita Castro); Leonard Gross, *The Last Best Hope: Eduardo Frei and Chilean Democracy* (New York: Random House, 1967), p. 112; cf. *Washington Post,* April 6, 1973, p. A12 (1964 Chile election).

33. *Human Events,* January 7, 1967.

34. Dr. Ochsner was one of the directors of Latin American Reports, Inc.,

International Trade Mart, New Orleans 16, Louisiana. Gaudet's reported admission "that he has in the past been an employee of CIA" (CD 75.588) does not of course link him to the CIA's anti-Castro operations. On the contrary, he wrote in a signed 1961 editorial that "we are going to have to live with Fidel Castro, and all he stands for in Cuba . . . Only in the remote event that Russia would establish a military base on the island, or that Castro would make an overt assault on a neighboring republic, would we have justification for direct intervention." (*Latin American Report*, August 1961)

However, there are at least two reasons why future investigators might wish to interview Mr. Gaudet, who is now retired.

(a) The FBI agent who interviewed Gaudet, SA John William Miller, filed a separate report the same day that "Gaudet telephonically contacted this agent to advise that he had heard Jack Ruby from Dallas, Texas, had purchased paintings from one Lorenzo Borenstein" (CD 4.644, at 26 H 337). Borenstein reportedly is a close relative of Leon Trotsky. Although Borenstein confirmed that Jack Ruby had bought several cheap paintings in 1959 (26 H 336), Gaudet has since denied giving Miller this information, which in retrospect looks like someone's flimsy effort to suggest an Oswald-Ruby-Trotskyite nexus.

(b) The Mexican government, in transmitting the names of the travelers whose permits immediately preceded and succeeded Oswald's, omitted one name—Gaudet's—from the sequence (24 H 679, 685). At least one other document transmitted at this time, a Mexican bus manifest with the name "OSWALD" on it (25 H 736, 24 H 673, 682), was found to have been altered by a member of the Office of the Mexican President (24 H 621-22, 25 H 599, 646); Oswald was later placed by the Warren Report on a different bus (R 736).

In like manner Gaudet is not mentioned anywhere in the extensive but ill-fated efforts by Jim Garrison to link the CIA through Oswald to the John F. Kennedy assassination. Regardless of the personal motives of the New Orleans district attorney and his volunteer staff, there are many grounds for thinking that the Garrison investigation was turned into an elaborate and successful disinformation effort. And two of the three financial sponsors of Garrison (Cecil Shilstone and Willard Robertson of Truth and Consequences, Inc.) had earlier been charter members of INCA along with Gaudet's sponsor, Dr. Alton Ochsner.

35. The four are Carlos J. Bringuier, Manuel Gil, Eduardo Guevara, and CRC head Luis Rabel Nunez (all Cubans). All but Bringuier were charter members of INCA.

36. At the William B. Reily Company, Inc., coffee merchants (R 726). H. Eustis Reily was an International Director of INCA. William B. Reily was a CRC financial patron recruited by the CRC's registered agent Ronny Caire: Milton E. Brener, *The Garrison Case: A Study in the Abuse of Power* (New York: Clarkson N. Potter, 1969), p. 47. Both men were officers of the William B. Reily Co., while Ronald Caire also "seemed to recall Oswald applying for a job" with him (22 H 831).

37. In addition one of Oswald's cousins had worked with the William B.

Reily Co. (26 H 764); and he had "some responsible position in one of the military reserve units" (23 H 718).

38. U.S., Cong., House, Committee on Armed Services, *Inquiry into the Alleged Involvement of the Central Intelligence Agency in the Watergate and Ellsberg Matters, Hearings,* 94th Cong, 1st Sess. (Washington: Government Printing Office, 1975), hereafter cited as Nedzi Hearings, pp. 945, 956, 1023. Three days after the Watergate break-in, Lee R. Pennington drove out to McCord's house and helped destroy incriminating material, including "something that had CIA on it" (p. 1025). Cf. J. Anthony Lukas, *Nightmare: The Underside of the Nixon Years* (New York: Viking, 1976), p. 211.

39. William W. Turner, *Power on the Right* (Berkeley: Ramparts Press, 1971), p. 188. A conference organized by Butler in 1970 featured as speaker Luis Kutner, who in 1963 had claimed to have intervened for Ruby with the Kefauver Committee: Turner, p. 188 (Butler-Kutner); Peter Dale Scott, "From Dallas to Watergate," in Scott, Hoch, and Stetler, p. 369 (Kutner-Ruby).

40. *San Francisco Chronicle,* November 26, 1975, p. 44 (payoffs); *San Francisco Chronicle,* June 6, 1974 (Torrijos-Standard Fruit); Horace Sutton, "The Curious Intrigues of Cuban Miami," *Saturday Review/World,* September 11, 1973, reprinted in Scott, Hoch, and Stetler, p. 402 (Torrijos-Hunt-Sturgis).

41. Stanley Penn, "On the Waterfront," in Nicholas Gage, ed., *Mafia: U.S.A.* (New York: Dell, 1972), p. 323.

42. *Victory* (New Orleans: INCA), March 3, 1965 (INCA-Weiss); Hank Messick, *Lansky* (New York: Putnam, 1971), pp. 83, 87 (Lansky-Weiss-Marcello). Messick notes that Weiss "became a leader in the fight against the 'international Communist conspiracy' " (p. 83).

43. Interview with former CIA official (Hunt); IV Congreso Continental Anticomunista, *Actas* (Guatemala, 1961), p. 415 (Antonio Valladares y Aycinena); *Saturday Evening Post,* February 29, 1964, p. 19 (Valladares-Marcello).

44. *Actas,* p. 417; William Turner, "The Garrison Commission," *Ramparts* (January 1968), reprinted in Scott, Hoch, and Stetler, p. 283.

45. The North American Congress on Latin America (NACLA) has charged that U.S. ambassador to Mexico Thomas C. Mann "figured in the planning" of this coup, which Kennedy declined to recognize; Susanne Jonas and David Tobis, eds., *Guatemala* (Berkeley: NACLA, 1974), p. 68n. Shortly thereafter it was announced that Mann was expected to retire as soon as a current matter of U.S.-Mexican negotiation was completed (*Christian Science Monitor,* June 29, 1963, p. 3). Yet Mann, who "requested that the investigation of 'D' 's claim be given the highest priority" (SHR, p. 42, cf. 5 H 366) was instead promoted under Lyndon Johnson to become the Assistant Secretary of State for Inter-American Affairs, and later Under-Secretary of State (cf. Scott, "The Death of Kennedy and the Vietnam War," p. 167).

46. Unpublished interview by Assistant New Orleans D.A. Jim Alcock with Alberto Fowler of the CRC and Laureano Batista of the MDC, February 5, 1967.

47. U.S., Cong., Senate, Committee on Government Operations, *Organized Crime: Stolen Securities, Hearings,* 92nd Cong., 1st Sess. (Washington: Govern-

ment Printing Office, 1971), pp. 685, 695-96, 713. Cited hereafter as Stolen Securities Hearings.

48. *Miami Herald,* July 17, 1971; Clark R. Mollenhoff, *Strike Force: Organized Crime and the Government* (Englewood Cliffs, N.J.: Prentice Hall, 1972), pp. 219-20 (Picture Island indictments); Jeff Gerth, "Nixon and the Mafia," *Sundance* (November-December 1972), reprinted in Steve Weissman, ed., *Big Brother and the Holding Company* (Palo Alto, Ca.: Ramparts Press, 1974), pp. 258, 261 (Salley and Roman).

49. George Crile III, *Washington Post,* May 2, 1976, p. C1.

50. Stolen Securities Hearings, p. 385; Gerth, pp. 259, 261; *Miami Herald,* September 18, 1949.

51. Scott, "From Dallas to Watergate," in Scott, Hoch, and Stetler, p. 373.

52. CD 984B.20; *Parade Magazine,* May 14, 1961; Scott, "The Death of Kennedy and the Vietnam War," p. 164.

52a. In August 1963 a violently anti-Castro exile group called MIRR took credit for a similar plane raid over the Shell refinery in Havana. (*Miami Herald,* August 17, 1963, p. A2) Manuel Gil of INCA, the CRC, and the Oswald-Bringuier debate is said to have joined the MIRR sometime after the Kennedy assassination (*New Orleans States Item,* February 20, 1967, quoted in H. Weisberg, *Oswald in New Orleans* [New York: Canyon Books, 1967], p. 362).

The MIRR's leader, Orlando Bosch, has also been involved in the anti-Castro raids of other activists to whom the false stories about the assassination and Lee Harvey Oswald were attributed—notably Frank Sturgis and his mercenary associate Jerry Buchanan (cf. CD 1020, Scott, Hoch, and Stetler, pp. 360-61).

In October 1976, Orlando Bosch was being sought for his role in a Cuban airline explosion in which seventy-three people were killed; Bosch reportedly also disclosed that two of his sometime Cuban exile associates were involved in the assassination of former Chilean foreign minister Orlando Letelier (*San Francisco Chronicle,* October 19, 1976, p. 14).

53. *San Francisco Chronicle,* May 4, 1963, p. 27.

54. *Hispanic American Report,* October 1963, p. 761 (Somoza meeting); CD 770.9 (de Leon on Oswald).

55. Two witnesses reported that Oswald on meeting Bringuier "asked him some questions like was he connected with the Cosa Nostra" (10 H 77, cf. 84), which may explain why Bringuier had the "feeling" on that day that maybe Oswald was from the FBI (10 H 35).

56. SHR, p. 78, citing CIA Inspector General's Report of 1967, p. 103.

57. The key Jack Anderson columns are those of March 3 and March 7, 1967, and January 18 and 19, 1971; his sources (John Roselli; his lawyer, Edward P. Morgan; and CIA officer William Harvey) are revealed in his subsequent column of September 9, 1976.

58. Assassination Report, p. 97, citing CIA Inspector General's Report, pp. 18-19.

59. George Crile III, *Washington Post,* May 16, 1971, p. C1 (Aleman); Stolen Securities Hearings, p. 686 ("Taylor"); Michael C. Jensen, *The Financiers: The*

World of the Great Wall Street Investment Banking Houses (New York: Weybright and Talley, 1976), pp. 268-74 (securities-narcotics).

60. The Senate Narcotics Hearings of 1964 named various Corsicans as narcotics traffickers, including Ansan Albert Bistoni, Jean Baptiste Croce and Paul Damien Mondoloni, who had continued to operate their Havana casinos under Castro: U.S., Cong., Senate, Committee on Government Operations, *Organized Crime and Illicit Traffic in Narcotics, Hearings,* 88th Cong., 2nd Sess. (Washington: Government Printing Office, 1964), pp. 954-55, 958. The CIA itself, through its French double agent P. L. Thyraud de Vosjoli, was drawing intelligence from de Vosjoli's French sources in Cuba: P. L. Thyraud de Vosjoli, *Lamia* (Boston: Little Brown, 1970), pp. 278-97. A French national, Pierre Owen Diez de Ure, was arrested in Havana on September 28, 1963 for his part in the plot of that month to assassinate Fidel Castro by blowing up the sewage pipes of the Presidential Palace: Press Release of July 30, 1975 from the office of Senator George McGovern, concerning Report from Cuban Government on the CIA in Cuba; cf. *Washington Post,* July 31, 1975, p. A1.

61. Crile, *Washington Post,* May 16, 1976, p. C1.

62. *San Francisco Chronicle,* July 10, 1976, p. 6.

63. Andrew St. George, *True,* August 1974; *New York News,* April 24, 1975; Robert K. Brown, "The Bayo-Pawley Affair," *Soldier of Fortune,* pp. 18, 21.

64. U.S. Department of State, *Bulletin,* April 22, 1963, pp. 600-601 (Joint Statement of March 30, 1963 by State and Justice Departments, quoted in Scott, "The Death of Kennedy and the Vietnam War," p. 161).

65. *New York Times,* September 16, 1963, p. 39.

66. "Operation Eagle" of June 1970, in which the BNDD arrested 130 members of a nationwide drug network, netted several high-level CIA Cuban protégés, including Bay of Pigs leader Jorge Alonso Pujol and Juan Cesar Restoy. Attorney-General John Mitchell called the group "a nationwide ring of wholesalers handling about 30 percent of all heroin sales and 75 to 80 percent of all cocaine sales in the United States": *New York Times,* June 22, 1970, p. 1; cf. *New York Times,* January 4, 1975, p. 8; Scott and Sutton, in Scott, Hoch, and Stetler, pp. 371, 395.

67. Szulc, *Compulsive Spy,* p. 97.

68. *Reno Evening Gazette,* January 8, 1975, p. 1.

69. Alfred W. McCoy, *The Politics of Heroin in Southeast Asia* (New York: Harper and Row, 1972), p. 27; Peter Dale Scott, *The War Conspiracy* (New York: Bobbs Merrill, 1972), p. 212; Andrew Tully, *The Secret War Against Dope* (New York: Coward, McCann and Geoghegan, 1973), p. 261. Tully calls Trafficante the "purported heir to the global syndicate established by Lucky Luciano and Meyer Lansky."

70. Crile, *Washington Post,* May 16, 1976.

71. Ibid.

72. *New York Times,* April 12, 1964, p. 1; cf. Sheridan, pp. 217, 356, 406-8.

73. Robert Kennedy, *The Enemy Within* (New York: Popular Library, 1960), pp. 228, 240-41. Robert Kennedy told how the McClellan Committee, for which he was majority counsel, searched for Giancana for fifteen months before finding him in Las Vegas.

74. Clark Mollenhoff relates that Hoffa "had a few [Michigan] federal judges in his pocket as a result of the days when Teamsters lawyer, George Fitzgerald, was Democratic National Committeeman from Michigan. These indications were strong enough to dissuade the Justice Department from trying to bring Hoffa to trial in that jurisdiction." Similar difficulties in Florida and Illinois led Kennedy "to bring the first action against the Teamsters boss in the Middle District of Tennessee" (Mollenhoff, *Strike Force,* p. 222).

Before the McClellan Committee Fitzgerald represented both Hoffa and Robert "Barney" Baker, the Teamster hoodlum whom (as we shall see) Jack Ruby phoned shortly before the Kennedy assassination (25 H 244).

75. Assassination Report, pp. 76-77.

76. Ibid., pp. 79, 133; cf. Ovid Demaris, *Captive City* (New York: Pocket Books, 1970), pp. 173-78.

77. Robert Sam Anson, *They've Killed the President* (New York: Bantam, 1975), pp. 295-96.

78. U.S., Cong., Senate, Select Committee on Improper Activities in the Labor or Management Field, *Hearings,* 85th Cong., 2nd Sess. (Washington: Government Print Office, 1959), hereafter cited as McClellan Hearings, e.g., pp. 15247-49, 19672-74.

79. Edward P. Morgan so identified himself on the CBS Evening News, August 22, 1976; cf. *Washington Post,* August 22, 1976, p. A1.

80. Jack Anderson later noted Pearson's "close personal friendship to Warren" (*New York Post,* September 7, 1976); he did not mention the longtime relationship between Morgan and himself, Pearson and Greenspun. Cf. infra.

81. Memorandum from FBI Washington Field Office to FBI Headquarters, March 21, 1967; SHR, p. 84.

82. Assassination Report, p. 174; SHR, pp. 83, 85, 105; Anderson, *New York Post,* September 9, 1976.

83. *San Francisco Chronicle,* March 3, 1967, p. 41.

84. Drew Pearson, *Diaries 1949-1959* (New York: Holt, Rinehart & Winston, 1974), pp. 167-68; Richard M. Fried, *Men Against McCarthy* (New York: Columbia University Press, 1976), pp. 78-79, 86, 225, etc.

85. Oliver Pilat, *Drew Pearson: An Unauthorized Biography* (New York: Pocket Books, 1973), p. 85.

86. Pilat, pp. 264-67; cf. Roger Hilsman, *To Move a Nation* (Garden City, N.Y.: Doubleday, 1967), pp. 346-57.

87. Pilat, pp. 275-76.

88. Reid, *Grim Reapers,* p. 142 (Davidson); Bobby Baker Hearings, pp. 1126, 1203, 2231-33 (Kampelman); cf. *Washington Observer,* December 15, 1966 (Anderson).

89. Pilat, pp. 274-75; *New York Times,* March 3, 1967, pp. 10-11. Inside the

government, now increasingly split between hawks and doves, a proponent of cautious bombing suspension was Pearson's close friend Leonard Marks, a co-owner of the Pearson column: *Pentagon Papers* (Boston: Beacon Press, 1972), v. IV, p. 142.

90. Jack Anderson, *San Francisco Chronicle,* January 18, 1971, p. 39, and January 19, 1971, p. 33; Scott, Hoch, and Stetler, pp. 375-80.

91. Memorandum from John Dean to H. R. Haldeman, January 26, 1971, in U.S., Cong., Senate, Select Committee on Presidential Campaign Activities, *Hearings,* 93rd Cong., 2nd Sess. (Washington: Government Printing Office, 1974), hereafter cited as Wat, Book 21, pp. 9751-53.

92. Memorandum from Jack Caulfield to John Dean, February 1, 1971, in 21 Wat 9755; cf. 9723.

93. Hunt, *Give Us This Day,* pp. 14-15, in Scott, Hoch, and Stetler, p. 381. Hunt's assassination proposal, despite his indication to the contrary, was "integral" to the Bay of Pigs blueprint: Richard Harris Smith (a former CIA officer), *Los Angeles Times,* December 5, 1975, II, p. 7; cf. Assassination Report, p. 127. In a J. Edgar Hoover memo of April 10, 1962, a senior CIA official alludes to the CIA-Mafia plot as "most sensitive information relating to the abortive Cuban invasion in April 1961" (Assassination Report, p. 131). This language, consistent with the CIA policy of never mentioning assassination on paper (cf. Assassination Report, p. 162), might seem to prefigure President Nixon's fatal remarks of June 23, 1972:

> We protected Helms from one hell of a lot of things. . . . Of course, this Hunt, that will uncover a lot of things. You open that scab there's a hell of a lot of things. . . . say, "Look the problem is that this will open the whole, the whole Bay of Pigs thing . . . very bad to have this fellow Hunt, ah, he knows too damned much, if he was involved—you happen to know that? If it gets out that this is all involved, the Cuba thing, it would be a fiasco. It would make the CIA look bad, it's going to make Hunt look bad, and it is very likely to blow the whole Bay of Pigs thing which we think would be very unfortunate—both for CIA and for the country, at this time, and for American foreign policy . . . the problem is it tracks back to the Bay of Pigs. (White House Edited Transcripts of June 23, 1972, in U.S., Cong., House, Committee on the Judiciary, *Hearings Pursuant to H. Res. 803:* Statement of Information [Washington: Government Printing Office, 1974], hereafter cited as Imp, Appendix III, pp. 43-44, 54, 75, 78; reprinted in New York Times, *The End of a Presidency* [New York: Bantam, 1974], pp. 330, 335-36, 347-48.)

In his book Watergate Minority Counsel Fred D. Thompson links this concern of the President to John Ehrlichman's statement in a private interview that Helms had declined to give him "a report of a secret in-house investigation on the CIA's role in the Bay of Pigs," and later, after Nixon's direct request, still delivered only part of the report: Fred D. Thompson, *At That Point in Time: The Inside Story of the Senate Watergate Committee* (New York: Quadrangle/New York Times

Book Co., 1975), p. 175. This report is presumably not that of the three-member Taylor Board which reviewed the Bay of Pigs disaster: that investigation was not in-house, and the report had already been delivered to the White House. It could well be the Inspector-General's Report of 1967, which was prepared in portions and apparently reported orally by Helms to President Johnson *before* the report was complete (SHR, p. 86). The Schweiker-Hart Subcommittee heard Helms "testify that he did not brief President Johnson about the 1964 and 1965 phases [of the AMLASH operation] because he did not regard AMLASH as an assassination agent" (SHR, p. 86). If the Inspector-General's Report is that alluded to by Ehrlichman, then "Bay of Pigs" may well have been in the Nixon White House, as in Hoover's memo ten years earlier, an acceptable euphemism for "assassination plots."

It is important to remember that Nixon was the original proponent of strong action against Castro, was the White House action officer on the project, and through his assistant Robert Cushman had an independent back channel to assassination proponent Howard Hunt (Nixon, p. 379; Hunt, pp. 39-40).

94. Daniel Schorr, *Rolling Stone,* April 8, 1976, p. 32.

95. Sheridan, p. 404; cf. pp. 364, 443-44, 431.

96. Ibid, p. 403; SHR, p. 105.

97. Sheridan, p. 488.

98. Edward Jay Epstein, *Counterplot* (New York: Viking, 1969), pp. 41-42; Sheridan, pp. 408-505, passim. The vice-president of Russell Long's Win Or Lose Corporation, a conduit for oil company payoffs, was Seymour Weiss, the INCA friend of Lansky: Ovid Demaris, *Dirty Business* (New York: Harper's, 1974), p. 199; T. Harry Williams, *Huey Long* (New York: Bantam, 1970), pp. 866-68.

99. Sheridan, p. 417; *Life,* September 1, 1967, p. 22; *Look,* August 26, 1969.

100. In June 1967, a Baton Rouge radio station carried the following story: "We can report that Edward G. Partin has been under investigation by the New Orleans District Attorney's Office in connection with the Kennedy assassination investigation . . . based on an exclusive interview with an Assistant District Attorney in Jim Garrison's office. We can report that Partin's activities have been under scrutiny. In his words: 'We know that Jack Ruby and Lee Harvey Oswald were here in New Orleans several times . . . there was a third man driving them and we are checking the possibility it was Partin' " (quoted in Sheridan, p. 423).

101. Foreign Lobbyist Hearings, pp. 1587, 1690; *New York Times,* September 28, 1963, p. 8.

102. Radio Station WINS, March 3, 1967, as reported in *New York World-Journal-Tribune,* March 4, 1967, quoted in Harold Weisberg, *Oswald in New Orleans,* p. 257: "Four Cuban assassination *teams* were organized"; cf. SHR, p. 84 (FBI blind memo of interview with Edward P. Morgan, March 21, 1967): "Castro . . . employed *teams* . . . who were dispatched to the United States"; 22 H 864 (FBI memo of May 8, 1964, discussed in Weisberg): "Pascual Enrique Ruedolo Gongora . . . stated that he was one of five or six *groups* sent to the United States to assassinate President Kennedy at the direction of Fidel Castro." Weisberg per-

suasively traces the WINS story to the long-discredited story of Gongora, a mental patient; and correctly points out that Garrison attributed the killing to the CIA, not to Castro. But not all of Garrison's team hewed to this line: for example, his prize witness, Perry Russo, soon called Garrison's prime suspect, David Ferrie, a "Marxist" follower of Che Guevara ("Russo Says: David W. Ferrie Was a Marxist," *Councilor* [Shreveport, La.], June 15, 1967; cited in Epstein, p. 169).

103. *Wall Street Journal,* July 31, 1972, p. 1; J. Anthony Lukas, "High Rolling in Las Vegas," *More,* May 1974, pp. 14-15.

104. John Keats, *Howard Hughes* (New York: Pyramid Books, 1970), p. 329; Omar Garrison, *Howard Hughes in Las Vegas* (New York: Dell, 1970), p. 40, says the negotiations between the Hughes representatives and Moe Dalitz "were climaxed on March 22, 1967."

105. Jack Anderson owned a small piece of Greenspun's newspaper (Lukas, *Nightmare,* p. 179); Greenspun had been a good friend of Pearson, Morgan and Anderson since the four of them successfully challenged the old McCarran-Joe McCarthy bloc in Congress (*More,* May 1974, p. 14; Pilat, p. 35; Hank Greenspun, *Where I Stand* [New York: David McKay, 1966], pp. 256-64). It was a message from Greenspun via Morgan to Hughes that started Hughes buying casinos in Las Vegas and putting them in the charge of Maheu, whose Washington office suite (900 17th St., Suite 316) was right next to Morgan's (900 17th St., Suite 300): *More,* May 1974, p. 14.

106. *San Francisco Chronicle,* March 1, 1976, p. 5 (Greenspun); *New York Times,* March 2, 1976, p. 10 (Anderson).

107. Keats, p. 329.

108. *Time,* December 21, 1970, p. 63 (Roselli); Omar Garrison, pp. 48-49, 56, 58 (Cohen and Entratter).

109. *Time,* December 21, 1970, p. 63; cf. *Wall Street Journal,* July 31, 1972, p. 21.

110. Lukas, *More,* May 1974, p. 15; cf. *Wall Street Journal,* July 31, 1972, p. 21.

111. *Wall Street Journal,* July 31, 1972, p. 21; 23 H 77 (Simmons-Ruby).

112. *Washington Observer,* April 15, 1967.

113. *Philadelphia Inquirer,* December 18-23, 1975; *Time,* April 19, 1976, p. 23.

114. For the Maheu-Intertel turnover, cf. Howard Kohn, "Strange Bedfellows: The Hughes-Nixon-Lansky Connection," *Rolling Stone,* May 20, 1976, pp. 83-84; Lukas, *Nightmare,* pp. 181-83; U.S., Cong., Senate, Select Committee on President Campaign Activities of 1972, unpublished staff report.

115. "It is clear that Mr. Greenspun secured a very favorable loan from the Hughes organization, a loan General Motors couldn't have gotten at any bank, while Mr. Maheu was in control of them" (*Wall Street Journal,* June 31, 1972, p. 21). Cf. Omar Garrison, p. 106, for the analogous case of Las Vegas banker E. Parry Thomas, another beneficiary of the Teamsters Pension Fund, who in addition received a finder's fee for the sale of the Sands to Hughes/Maheu.

115a. *New York Times,* June 28, 1976, p. 20.

116. U.S., Cong., Senate, Select Committee on Presidential Campaign Activities, *Final Report,* 93rd Cong., 2nd Sess., Report No. 93-981 (Washington: Government Printing Office, 1974), hereafter cited as Watergate Report, Appendix to Views of Senator Baker, hereafter cited as Baker Report, pp. 1121-26; cf. p. 1161; reprinted in *The Senate Watergate Report* (New York: Dell, 1974), hereafter cited as Wat. Rep. (Dell), v. I, pp. 737-40. Cf. Memorandum of March 1, 1973, to CIA Deputy Director for Plans from CIA Chief/Central Cover Staff, reprinted in Nedzi Committee Hearings, pp. 1073-76: "Mr. Bennett said also that he has been feeding stories to Bob Woodward of the *Washington Post* with the understanding that there be no attribution to Bennett. Woodward is suitably grateful for the fine stories and by-lines which he gets and protects Bennett (and the Mullen Company). . . . he stated his opinion that the Ervin Committee investigating the Watergate incident would not involve the company. He said that, if necessary, he could have his father, Senator Bennett of Utah, intercede with Senator Ervin. His conclusion then was he could handle the Ervin Committee if the Agency can handle Howard Hunt" (pp. 1074-75). Howard Kohn is one of the few Watergate journalists to discuss this so-called Eisenstadt memorandum: *Rolling Stone,* May 20, 1976, p. 88. The accounts by Anthony Lukas and by Elizabeth Drew, excellent in other respects, pass over this memo in silence.

117. Noah Dietrich and Bob Thomas, *Howard: The Amazing Mr. Hughes* (Greenwich, Conn.: Fawcett, 1972), pp. 260-61.

118. Dietrich and Thomas, pp. 266-68; Larry DuBois and Laurence Gonzales, "The Puppet and the Puppetmasters," *Playboy,* September 1976, p. 180.

119. *Time,* April 19, 1976, p. 23.

120. *Miami Herald,* August 25, 1963; *Hispanic American Report,* December 1963, p. 1153; CD 1085 D10.2; *Playboy,* September 1976, p. 180.

121. *Playboy,* September 1976, p. 183.

122. The Hughes-TWA suit alone ran up legal fees estimated at over $22 million (James R. Phelan, "Howard Hughes, Beyond the Law," *New York Times Magazine,* September 14, 1975, p. 48). Of this sum about two thirds, or roughly $15 million, was earned by Hughes attorneys—chiefly Chester C. Davis and senior partners of OSS-Chief Donovan's law firm, Donovan, Leisure, Newton and Irvine.

123. Phelan, *New York Times Magazine,* September 14, 1975, p. 48.

124. *New York Times,* April 8, 1975, p. 9.

125. James Kirkwood, *American Grotesque* (New York: Simon & Schuster, 1968), p. 162; James Phelan, "Rush to Judgment in New Orleans," *Saturday Evening Post,* May 6, 1967, p. 21; Epstein, *Counterplot,* pp. 66-70; Anson, p. 115: "The first major blow came from James Phelan . . ."

126. Stephen Fay, Lewis Chester, and Magnus Linklater, *Hoax: The Inside Story of the Howard Hughes-Clifford Irving Affair* (New York: Viking, 1972), p. 115; cf. James Phelan, *Playboy,* December 1971 (Mormons); Lukas, *More,* May 1974, p. 28 (Greenspun).

127. *Washington Observer,* May 1, 1971. Two other journalists who figure more prominently in the Lee Harvey Oswald story have also contributed to the public image of a living Howard Hughes. Aline Mosby, who reportedly inter-

viewed Oswald in Moscow (R 256, 259), is also reportedly one of the last journalists to have been granted an interview by Howard Hughes, according to Hughes's first biographer, John Keats (Keats, pp. 268-70). Tommy Thompson, the mysterious *Time-Life* man who hid Marguerite and Marina Oswald from press and police on the night of November 23, 1963 (1 H 151-52; cf. *Life*, November 29, 1963, p. 37), was (according to James Phelan) the real author of the Keats biography. Phelan quotes Keats as saying, "My role was confined to that of car washer. . . . The book was really written by another man" *Reporter*, July 14, 1966, p. 58.

128. *New York Times*, February 11, 1972, p. 30 (Maheu), February 14, 1972, pp. 1, 20 (Phelan); Fay et al., p. 202 (Vietnam). By contrast the Watergate break-in had so little impact on the 1972 election because fewer than fifteen reporters were assigned full-time to cover it, out of four hundred thirty-three reporters in the sixteen largest Washington newspaper bureaus (Lukas, *Nightmare*, p. 275). In January 1972 the *Los Angeles Times* alone had nine men on the Clifford Irving story (Fay et al., p. 202). Maheu knew Irving's lawyer Martin Ackerman, and had contacted him in 1968 when Ackerman was president of the company which had published Phelan's story debunking Garrison, about purchasing the *Saturday Evening Post*. This company, Curtis Publishing, was for some reason telephoned by Jack Ruby shortly before the Kennedy assassination (25 H 238, 240), at which time it employed the moderator of the Oswald-Butler debate (CD 351).

128a. IRS Commissioner Walters, Notes for Briefing, March 3, 1972; *Hoax*, pp. 124-26.

129. Fay et al., *Hoax*, pp. 124, 137 (Richard Hannah of Carl Byoir and Associates), pp. 172-76, 197, 232 (Intertel), pp. 215-22 (Phelan); 20 Wat 9367, Baker Report, in Wat. Rep. (Dell), p. 738: "Bennett asked for and received from Hunt a price estimate for bugging Clifford Irving for Hughes"; cf. Thompson, p. 149.

130. Fay et al., *Hoax*, pp. 115-19, 216-22; *New York Times*, February 14, 1972, pp. 1, 20. The Irving-Phelan parallels in *Hoax* (pp. 220-22) indicate that the Phelan manuscript, despite implications to the contrary, was substantially that published the next month (by Phelan's contact at Fawcett, Ralph Daigh [*Hoax*, p. 262]) as *Howard* by Noah Dietrich and Bob Thomas, with "preliminary research . . . by James Phelan" (p. 11). Three examples will serve for the rest:

Phelan ms. (= Irving)	Dietrich
When people walk in the hangar for the first time they are *overwhelmed*. They stand there with their mouths open and tilt their heads back until they are looking way up there at the top of the plane. Then they say, *"Jeeeeeeesus Chriiiiiiist!"* (*Hoax*, p. 221)	When people walk in the hangar for the first time they are *staggered*. They *just* stand there with their mouths open and tilt their heads back until they are looking way up there at the top of the plane. Then they say, *"Jeeeeezuzz Keeristt!"* (p. 171)

. . . kick Long Beach in the ass	. . . kick Long Beach in the ass
about the tideland oil settlement	*on* the tideland oil settlement
(*Hoax*, p. 222)	(p. 214)

"You can junk the plane now and	"You can junk the plane now and
nobody could possibly criticize	nobody could possibly criticize
(Irving: will criticize) you."	you."
(*Hoax*, p. 222)	(p. 213)

Cf. *Hoax*, p. 114: The Dietrich-Phelan "relationship had ended two years later without any book being published."

131. *New York Times*, February 4, 1972, p. 1; Wat. Rep. (Dell), p. 76; unpublished Ervin Committee report, p. 23 (*New York Times*, January 16, 17, and 24, 1972).

132. According to Dietrich and Thomas (i.e., Phelan), p. 285, "one month after the [1956 Hughes-Nixon] loan was made . . . the Internal Revenue Service made a reversal and ruled that the Howard Hughes Medical Foundation [since accused of being a CIA-front, cf. supra at notes 119-120] was entitled to tax-exempt status."

Cf. *New York Times*, August 4, 1975, p. 10: "Howard R. Hughes got his secret contract with the Central Intelligence Agency for the ship Glomar Explorer five weeks after making an 'emergency' contribution of $100,000 to President Nixon's 1972 re-election campaign, according to sources familiar with a tax investigation of the ship here."

133. Wat. Rep. (Dell), p. 71; 21 Wat 9899-9910, where Caulfield calls Intertel a "Kennedy mafia dominated intelligence 'gun for hire' " (p. 9900), with "potential . . . to be exposed as a mafia front" (p. 9901).

134. Unpublished Ervin Committee report, pp. 22-23.

135. 2 Wat 790; cf. 1 Imp 65; Jeb Stuart Magruder, *An American Life* (New York: Pocket Books, 1975), p. 212.

136. 20 Wat 9372, cf. 9369-70, 9377, 9 Wat 3686, and Nedzi Hearings, p. 1110. One of these problems, as we have just seen, was the Clifford Irving manuscript, 20 Wat 9367. But it is important to keep in mind that Greenspun and Anderson (another of the plumbers' targets, cf. Magruder, p. 206) also possessed at least some of the government documents recording Morgan's story of 1967 about Castro and the CIA-Mafia plot (*San Francisco Chronicle*, March 1, 1976, p. 5; *New York Post*, March 2, 1976).

137. Watergate Report (GPO), p. 936; Wat. Rep. (Dell), p. 434. Lukas, (*Nightmare*, p. 114) alleges that "negotiations foundered" after Rebozo failed to meet Morgan's conditions; and that "Morgan called the Hughes representatives and recommended against contributing to Nixon." There is nothing to support these claims in the published records of the Ervin Committee, which on the contrary document a series of checks from "Howard R. Hughes" (per his money-handler Lee Murrin) to Robert A. Maheu, for possible payment to Nixon, beginning July 30, 1968 (24 Wat 11526-35); cf. Watergate Report (GPO), p. 938.

The Ervin Committee, more interested in Nixon than in Hughes, published only the conflicting testimonies of Danner and Rebozo about the Hughes contribution, not the testimony of Robert Maheu and of Edward P. Morgan. It also declined to adjudicate the issue of whether Rebozo or the Hughes representatives initiated the discussions about the contribution. A Howard Hughes memo of March 14, 1968 to Robert Maheu (not mentioned in the report or published testimony) suggests that there was a Hughes initiative:

> I want you to go to see Nixon as my special confidential emissary. I feel there is a really valid possibility of a Republican victory this year. If that could be realized under our sponsorship and supervision every inch of the way, then we would be ready to follow with Laxalt as our next candidate. (26 Wat 12780; cf. Kohn, p. 82)

This instruction would explain why Morgan, according to Rebozo, "wanted to hand the money to the President himself" (21 Wat 9943; Lukas, *Nightmare,* p. 114). Rebozo refused, on the grounds that "Ed Morgan represented Drew Pearson," who in 1960 had exposed the 1956 Hughes-Nixon loan (p. 9943).

138. From Nixon's point of view, the damaging testimony from the two factions (Maheu-Morgan and Intertel-Hunt-Bennett) must have seemed like a single concerted campaign. On September 24, 1973, Hunt testified about his plans with Bennett and Liddy to burgle Hank Greenspun's safe. On September 25, a story about Hunt's testimony by John Hanrahan in the *Washington Post* recalled Jack Anderson's columns of 1971-72 about the $100,000 payment from Danner to Rebozo. It quoted from the March 1968 Hughes-Maheu memo and added information from Bennett to the *Post, prior* to Hunt's testimony, that "Rumors concerning Greenspun's memos led to the formulation of the break-in plan" (*Washington Post,* September 25, 1973, p. A18). Six days later, the *New York Times,* in an article by Greenspun's friend Wallace Turner, reported further details of Danner's delivery of the cash from the evidence presented by Robert Maheu on July 4 in his private suit against Hughes (*New York Times,* October 1, 1973, p. 28); cf. Elizabeth Drew, *Washington Journal: The Events of 1973-1974* (New York: Vintage, 1976), pp. 28-29. Subsequent testimony by Chester Davis ("Here's the goddam money," Drew, p. 141), by Robert Peloquin of Intertel, and by Robert Bennett all either corroborated Hunt's and/or Maheu's stories, or expanded upon them.

139. The *Miami News* of October 19, 1973 (p. 2A, in 21 Wat 10151) correctly reported that "Rebozo's handling of the Hughes cash" was being simultaneously investigated by Carmine Bellino and by Special Watergate Prosecutor Archibald Cox. (Rebozo's lawyer and Bellino have exchanged charges as to which of them was responsible for the leak, 21 Wat 10145, cf. Thompson, p. 187.) About the same time White House aide Alexander Haig, after a call from a Rebozo lawyer, complained to Attorney General Richardson about Cox's investigation of the Hughes contribution (23 Wat 11216). On October 20, in the so-called "Saturday night massacre," the White House announced the firing of Cox;

one of the many ensuing rumors was that "Cox was fired because he was looking into the financial affairs of Bebe Rebozo and the hundred-thousand-dollar payment from Hughes" (Drew, p. 80).

140. Cf. supra, note 22. Anderson's friends Davidson and Greenspun were also (like their friend Jimmy Hoffa) active in support of Israel—Davidson as a registered lobbyist for the Israeli munitions industry and Greenspun as a fund-raiser and former gun-runner for the Haganah.

141. The company was the Cuban-Venezuelan Oil Voting Trust (9 H 202), whose director Jose I. de la Camara was an employee of Agustin Batista Falla's Trust Company of Cuba. De Mohrenschildt, who claimed to have worked in World War II for French intelligence (9 H 183-84), also worked briefly in 1940 for his "distant cousin" Baron Constantine Maydell, then the top German Abwehr agent in the United States: 9 H 182; CD 533.8, 18, 58, 67; Ladislas Farago, *The Game of the Foxes* (New York: David McKay, 1971), p. 305.

142. The Russian Orthodox Church Outside Russia, subsidized through the CIA-conduit David, Josephine and Winifred Baird Foundation (for which cf. *New York Times*, March 5, 1967, p. 36). A House Select Committee chaired by Congressman Patman charged that the foundation's president, David Baird, "repeatedly violated Treasury regulations" by using his family foundations to buy and sell stock on behalf of speculators such as Henry Crown, Joseph Binns, Conrad Hilton, William Zeckendorf and Lou Chesler (U.S., Cong., House, Select Committee on Small Business, *Tax Exempt Foundations and Charitable Trusts*, Staff Report, Part II, 88th Cong., 1st Sess. [Washington: Government Printing Office, 1963]; *New York Times*, October 20, 1963, p. 77). A year after the CIA foundations revelations, the SEC closed its investigation into Baird, on the grounds that he was sick and retired, and his foundations inactive (*New York Times,* July 9, 1968, p. 57). Four years later an informant and colleague of Sam Benton identified Baird as a participant in a 1950s stock manipulation; another witness named Lou Chesler (Stolen Securities Hearings, pp. 645-46, 857).

143. Howard Kohn has alleged in *Rolling Stone* (May 20, 1976, p. 49) that Guy Banister, whose detective agency occupied the building with the 544 Camp Street address used by Oswald, had known Robert Maheu from their days together in the Chicago office of the FBI. Meanwhile, Walter Sheridan, in charging that the Garrison investigation of Oswald became an intrigue "intertwined" with efforts to save Hoffa and nail anti-Hoffa witness Partin (p. 417), focused on the harassment of Partin by another private detective, Joseph Oster of Southern Research, Inc. (Sheridan, pp. 440-42). Oster arrested Ed Partin on the basis of a complaint by photographer Irby Aucoin, who one year earlier, on the night of Clay Shaw's arrest, had brought an almost identical complaint against one of Shaw's friends (James and Wardlaw, p. 54). Sheridan does not mention that Oster was a former partner of Guy Banister, and a current partner of Milton Kaack, the former FBI agent who filed a pre-assassination report on Oswald's arrest in New Orleans, based on an FBI interview with Oswald at his own request (R 437; 17 H 753, 758).

144. Jack Anderson, *Washinton Expose* (Washington: Public Affairs Press, 1967), pp. 212-13.

145. The Secret Service had arranged a reservation for Marguerite and Marina Oswald at the motel by 11:00 a.m. on November 24, *before* Oswald was shot; even though their first excuse for this action (which had no standing authority to justify it) was a compassionate order from Lyndon Johnson *after* the assassination (CD 87, SS 533.1-2; cf. 1 H 471-72).

Marguerite Oswald and Peter Gregory (the parish organizer) later testified under oath that the Secret Service made the reservation at Marguerite's request, with Gregory, her new Russian instructor, as intermediary (1 H 155-56, 2 H 344). By a "very unusual coincidence" (1 H 155) Marguerite had begun to study Russian ten days before the assassination, with the man whose family (unbeknown to her) had helped support Lee and Marina when they first came from Russia to Fort Worth (2 H 340). Deciding that she needed "help" at 6:30 a.m. Sunday morning, she phoned her Russian instructor whose classes she had attended exactly twice, with several other women. It was thus completely by accident that Marguerite and Marina were sequestered for 36 hours from the FBI by Secret Service agent Mike Howard, who was already looking for them on Saturday night (16 H 902), and Peter Gregory, who had already been selected on Saturday, perhaps even on Friday (2 H 344, 23 H 421), to be Marina's interpreter.

Peter Gregory should be asked about his alteration in translation of Marina's testimony about the alleged murder rifle (CD 344.22-23), to supply details which at the same time were corroborated by another "interpreter" (co-founder with Gregory of the CIA-subsidized parish, 9 H 111, 121, 124), and by two warehouse employees of the Great Southwest Corporation, which owned the motel where Marina was hidden (26 H 370-72).

146. U.S., Cong., House, Committee on Banking and Currency, *The Penn Central Failure and the Role of Financial Institutions,* Staff Report, 91st Cong., 2nd Sess. (Washington: Government Printing Office, 1970), Part III, p. 30: Great Southwest Corporation control (in late 1963) "was tightly centered in the Rockefeller and Wynne families." Quotation also in Joseph R. Daughen and Peter Binzen, *The Wreck of the Penn Central* (New York: Signet, 1971), p. 135. The firm's real estate operations were later cited as a major factor in the bankruptcy of the Penn Central railroad (1970), and before it of William Zeckendorf's Webb & Knapp, once the largest single beneficiary of a Teamsters pension-fund loan.

147. Congressional Record, January 26, 1965, p. 1313; U.S., Cong., Senate, Committee on Rules, *Construction of the District of Columbia Stadium, Hearings,* 88th Cong., 2nd Sess. (Washington: Government Printing Office, 1964), pp. 859-87. Dallas Republican leader Robert H. Stewart III, a director of the Great Southwest Corporation and trustee of the Toddie Lee Wynne Foundation, had also arranged for questionable loans to Bobby Baker, via the same two Murchison representatives (Robert Thompson and Thomas Webb) who figured in the Baker payoffs from Bedford Wynne (Bobby Baker Hearings, pp. 987 ff.).

148. U.S., National Archives, Warren Commission conference with Isaac Don Levine, May 28, 1964, p. 2.

149. Drew Pearson, *Diaries 1949-1959* (New York: Holt, Rinehart and Winston, 1974), p. 255, cf. pp. 461-62: *"Life* magazine is always pulling chestnuts out of the fire for the CIA; and I recall that C. D. Jackson of the Life-Time

empire, was the man who arranged for the CIA to finance the Freedom Balloons. C. D. Jackson, Harold Stassen, and the other boys who went with me to Germany and spent money like money [sic], while I paid my own way. I always was suspicious that a lot of dough was coming from unexplained quarters and didn't learn until sometime later that the CIA was footing the bill."

150. U.S., National Archives, Warren Commission memorandum of February 28, 1964 from Norman Redlich.

151. Isaac Don Levine conference, May 28, 1964, p. 2.

152. CD 1039 records details of a short-lived contract between Martin and Charles William Deaton, a man with an FBI record and alleged links to the Smaldone family in Colorado. Martin knew Ruby on a first-name basis from the days when he was Credit Manager of the Statler-Hilton in Dallas, and later manager of the "Gay Nineties," a Dallas bottle club (CD 360.47, 49; CD 106.251; 2 H 20).

In October 1976 Deaton was in a West German jail awaiting extradition on U.S. charges he defrauded investors of over $30 million through a plan to extract gold and silver from worthless ore (*San Francisco Examiner,* October 17, 1976, p. A1). Deaton worked his scam out of the Castle Bank in the Bahamas, a high-level Mafia tax haven for Moe Dalitz and other members of the Cleveland Syndicate. IRS Commissioner Donald Alexander cut off an IRS investigation of the Castle Bank after it had turned up the name of Castle's Miami attorney, Paul L. E. Helliwell (a former OSS official who set up at least one CIA proprietary) and two members of Alexander's old law firm: Hank Messick, *Rolling Stone,* May 20, 1976, p. 51 (Castle); Scott, *War Conspiracy,* pp. 210-11 (Helliwell).

153. "Mrs. Ford: . . . I think Mr. McKenzie didn't know what they would talk about but he advised her, 'They will ask you if there were two guns, you tell them there was one gun that was used,' he told her" (2 H 321, cf. 336-37). Other parts of Mrs. Ford's testimony fix this conversation on February 18, 1964. An FBI report of an interview in McKenzie's office with Marina that day records that "Marina said to her knowledge Oswald had only one rifle and that rifle is the one he maintained in the Paine garage" (22 H 785).

154. Anderson, *Washington Expose,* pp. 212-13: "It was oil millionaire Clint Murchison's associate Bedford Wynn[e], who offered to stage a $1,000-a-plate Democratic dinner in January, 1963. The dinner raised $500,000, largely from oil men, to pay off the whopping 1960 Democratic debt. Shortly after the dinner, Clint Murchison's son, John, paid a private 90-minute call on the President [about proposed cuts in the oil depletion allowance] . . . and assured fellow oil men they had nothing to worry about." Cf. *World Petroleum* (April 1964), p. 4: "The threat to oil's income tax depletion allowance becomes less severe as President Kennedy says he's willing to settle for a tax cut, alone, without tax reforms."

155. *Wall Street Journal,* October 8, 1964, p. 16; Arlington, Texas, registry of land titles (real estate deal); Earl Mazo and Stephen Hess, *Nixon: A Political Portrait* (New York: Popular Library, 1968), p. 296 ("law business"); *Dallas Times-Herald,* November 21, 1963, in 23 H 941, "Nixon Here Before JFK on 'Business'." Just five days earlier, on November 15, Nixon had petitioned to join

the New York Bar (*Time,* November 22, 1963, p. 17). Subsequently, Nixon made two very political trips to Asia for Pepsico, making contact with powerful CIA-linked lobbies for U.S. intervention in Vietnam and possibly Indonesia: cf. Peter Dale Scott, *The War Conspiracy,* p. 168; Peter Dale Scott, "Opium and Empire," *Bulletin of Concerned Asian Scholars* (September 1973), p. 54; Peter Dale Scott, "Exporting Military-Economic Development: America and the Overthrow of Sukarno, 1965-67," in Malcolm Caldwell, ed., *Ten Years' Military Terror in Indonesia* (Nottingham, England: Spokesman Books, 1975), pp. 240-41.

156. Nixon (FBI), February 28, 1964: "Mr. NIXON advised that the *only* time he was in Dallas, Texas, during 1963 was *two days prior to* the assassination of President John F. Kennedy. He vaguely thought there was some *invitation* extended during the early part of 1963, probably in April, for him to come to Dallas, but it never materialized." (23 H 831)

Cf. McKenzie (Warren Commission), February 21, 1964: "Mr. Nixon did come to Dallas some time within 6 weeks *prior to* November 22, 1963. . . . I don't know exactly when it was, but I know it was *prior to* November 22d, Dick Nixon was in Dallas. . . . I recall when Mr. Nixon was coming to Dallas at the *invitation* of Mr. Carlson and others to receive this award." (1 H 339)

Maurice Carlson was president of a Wynne family insurance company (of which William McKenzie's law partner Henry Baer was secretary), whose building housed Dallas CIA representative J. Walton Moore and the Secret Service; Carlson was also a Dallas Republican Party official and "a close friend of Richard Nixon" (23 H 414). Carlson's claim to the FBI on February 19, 1964 about this Nixon "invitation" was in partial corroboration of William McKenzie's and Robert Oswald's story to the FBI (from Marina) that "Oswald intended to shoot Nixon" and "Marina had locked Lee Harvey Oswald in the bathroom the entire day that he planned to shoot Nixon to prevent him from doing so" (22 H 596; cf. 1 H 336-37). On February 24, when it was established that the Oswalds' bathroom (like most others) locked from the inside rather than the outside, Marina altered the story to make it even less credible: "she [i.e., Marina, a ninety-eight-pound pregnant woman] forcibly held the bathroom door shut holding on to the knob and bracing her feet against the wall" (23 H 511). Finally, she would tell the Warren Commission a third version, that she and her husband "struggled for several minutes . . . *in* the bathroom . . . when I collect all my forces and want to do something very badly I am stronger than he is" (5 H 388-89, cf. R 188).

However, Maurice Carlson, president of Reliance Life and Accident, *withdrew* his story about an invitation ("since refreshing his memory, he remembered it was Senator Barry Goldwater of Arizona and not Nixon," 23 H 416) on February 24, 1964, the day that McKenzie's partner Henry Baer, Secretary of Reliance Life and Accident, heard Marina tell her short-lived story about "holding on to the knob and bracing her feet" (23 H 511).

Since it is now conceded that there never was any invitation for Nixon to visit Dallas in April 1963, McKenzie, if not Nixon, should be asked what made him "recall" such an event.

157. Supra, at note 93.

158. *Playboy,* September 1976, p. 180; cf. supra, at note 120.

159. 24 Wat 11416, 11426, 26 Wat 12456 (Smathers); 24 Wat 11416 (David-son-Anderson); 24 Wat 11413, 11440, 20 Wat 9552, Wat. Rep. (Dell), p. 433 (Clint Murchison, Jr.). Before joining the Hughes operations Danner also saw a lot of Ed Morgan when Morgan was attorney for the shareholders of the Las Vegas Tropicana (including George Smathers, 24 Wat 11416), where a hidden interest was attributed to Carlos Marcello: Ed Reid and Ovid Demaris, *The Green Felt Jungle* (New York: Pocket Books, 1964), p. 71. It was Morgan who, after the 1968 election, suggested to Danner (an old friend of Nixon and Rebozo) that he should join the Hughes Nevada Operations under Maheu (24 Wat 11430, 11447).

160. Robert Kennedy, *The Enemy Within,* p. 87.

161. *Chicago Tribune,* December 9, 1939, p. 1.

162. McClellan Committee Hearings, pp. 16084-103.

163. 22 H 326, 366, 435; Demaris, *Captive City,* pp. 164, 361, 376.

164. 22 H 425. According to Barney Ross, the most successful boxer in the group, the gang sometimes used "to run innocuous errands for Al Capone" (22 H 422). Charles "Cherry Nose" Gioe, who was convicted with John Roselli in the 1943 Hollywood extortion case, also got his start in life as a "messenger boy" for Al Capone (5 Kefauver Hearings 536).

165. 5 Kefauver Hearings 682, 759, 955; cf. Gaeton Fonzi, *Annenberg: A Biography of Power* (New York: Weybright and Talley, 1970).

166. R 787; 22 H 349; 20 H 37, 58.

167. *San Francisco Chronicle,* September 26, 1974, p. 1; January 11, 1975, p. 5.

168. Scott, "From Dallas to Watergate," in Scott, Hoch, and Stetler, pp. 368-69; 22 H 372, 318; 5 Kefauver Hearings 461-65; Demaris, *Captive City,* p. 141.

169. Rufus King, *Gambling and Organized Crime* (Washington: Public Affairs Press, 1969), pp. 27-29. The Kefauver Committee heard the same message from wire-service veteran John Roselli: "The wire-service company never could get along without local corruption. You know that" (5 Kefauver Hearings 384).

170. Drew Pearson, *Diaries: 1949-1959,* p. 470 (Crown); Demaris, *Captive City,* pp. 243-49 (Crown-Arvey), 183 (quoting secret federal report of circa 1961): "Advised that Patrick could not be stopped in his gambling and other illicit activities since he was backed politically by Jake Arvey, Sidney Deutsch [former Finance Committee Chairman of the Cook County Board of Commis-sioners—deceased 1961], and Arthur X. Elrod [deceased 1959]. Advised that Patrick grew up in Arvey's ward and that Arvey would call upon him for strong arm tactics in connection with stuffing ballot boxes." Ruby himself was re-portedly (22 H 327), and his brother Hymie admittedly (15 H 11), active in the Arvey-Elrod political machine; cf. 21 H 314. Ruby later attributed his business interest in Cuba to the unrelated interests of the Arvey family in Cuba, which were not generally known: Melvin R. Belli and M. C. Carroll, *Dallas Justice: The Real Story of Jack Ruby and His Trial* (New York: David McKay, 1964), p. 48.

171. Reid and Demaris, *The Green Felt Jungle,* p. 192.

172. "Collier's Tip Sheet" (20 H 58, cf. 20 H 37; Fonzi, pp. 66-68).

173. Robert Blair Kaiser, *"R.F.K. Must Die!"* (New York: Grove Press, 1970), pp. 111, 292.

174. U.S., Cong., House, Committee on Government Operations, *Investigation As to the Manner in which the United States Board of Parole Is Operating and As to Whether There Is a Necessity for a Change in Either the Procedure or Basic Law, Hearings,* 80th Cong., 2nd Sess. (Washington: Government Printing Office, 1948), hereafter cited as Parole Board Hearings, pp. 561-62.

175. R 792-93; 22 H 300, 478.

176. *Chicago Tribune,* August 30, 1947, p. 3. The first post-assassination report of the government case file (from the Secret Service) agreed with Jones's account and unambiguously contradicted Ruby's (23 H 206). The Warren Report chose to cite this report, which appeared to exculpate Ruby (R 793 at note 245); in fact, it demolished Ruby's alibi.

177. 24 H 69; cf. Sylvia Meagher, *Accessories After the Fact: The Warren Commission, The Authorities and The Report* (New York: Vintage, 1976), pp. 423-25.

178. 5 Kefauver Hearings 1180; McClellan Hearings, pp. 12524-25.

179. 22 H 297; Reid and Demaris, *The Green Felt Jungle,* pp. 197-98.

180. Belli, p. 48; R. Hart Phillips, *Cuba: Island of Paradox* (New York: McDowell, Obolensky, 1959), p. 394; Herbert Matthews, *The Cuban Story* (New York: George Braziller, 1961), p. 87.

181. R 370, 802; Scott, "From Dallas to Watergate," in Scott, Hoch, and Stetler, p. 370.

182. *New York Daily News,* April 23, 1975; Anson, pp. 298, 309, 312.

183. CD 686d, reprinted in Michael Canfield and Alan J. Weberman, *Coup d'Etat in America* (New York: The Third Press, 1975), pp. 293-94. This FBI letterhead memorandum of March 26, 1964 contains information about McWillie "developed by the FBI in connection with another matter." It reveals that the FBI was interviewing Nevada authorities about McWillie on November 20, 1963 and November 21, 1963—just before the Kennedy assassination.

184. Messick, *Lansky,* p. 196, cf. McClellan Hearings, p. 12370 (Capri-Tourine); Hank Messick, *The Private Lives of Public Enemies* (New York: Dell, 1973), pp. 13-21 (Tourine-Ilona Lorenz); *Los Angeles Times,* June 13, 1976, p. 5; June 15, 1976, p. 18: "Fiorini . . . said he first persuaded her [Ilona Lorenz] to photograph Castro's secret papers, later helped her escape from Cuba and supplied her with the poison."

185. 23 H 165 (McWillie-Cal Neva); Demaris, *Captive City,* p. 12 (Cal-Neva–Giancana).

186. Sam Giancana's presence with Frank Sinatra at the Cal Neva in July 1963 was revealed in a complaint of September 11, 1963 by the Chairman of the Nevada Gaming Control Board (Reid and Demaris, *The Green Felt Jungle,* p. 198). This highly publicized revelation about Giancana at Cal Neva may well have led to the FBI's request for McWillie's Cal Neva work card on November 20, 1963 (CD 686d, in Canfield and Weberman, p. 294).

187. McClellan Hearings, pp. 12522, 12525.

188. 23 H 363; cf. Chicago Crime Commission, 1958 Report, p. 47; U.S., Cong., Senate, *Gambling and Organized Crime,* Senate Report 1310, 87th Cong., 2nd Sess. (Washington: Government Printing Office, 1962), pp. 45, 47, hereafter cited as Gambling Report.

189. 22 H 423, cf. CD 1193.69-75 (Ruby-Kopple); Chicago Crime Commission, 1966 Report, p. 119 (1966 arrest).

190. Gambling Report, pp. 45, 760-71 (Beckley-betting); Stolen Securities Hearings, p. 713, Mollenhoff, *Strike Force,* p. 31 (Beckley-securities).

191. Chicago Crime Commission, 1966 Report, p. 118 (Caesar's Palace, Frank Rosenthal); Reid, *Grim Reapers,* pp. 232-33 (Giancana); *Overdrive,* January 1973, p. 82 (Allan Dorfman, Jay Sarno, Frank Rosenthal, Hank Greenspun).

192. Scott, in Scott, Hoch, and Stetler, pp. 368-69; 25 H 294-95; McClellan Hearings, pp. 7416, 18308, 18815 (local 320).

193. 12 H 160, 23 H 40, 23 H 78 ("Cavagnaro stated Ruby was well acquainted with a great number of policemen and particularly the policemen who were in or had been in the Special Service of the Police. He stated that he knew Ruby was a close friend of Lieutenant Gilmore and Eric Kaminski");23 H 207, 25 H 228-29, 25 H 290; cf. Scott, in Scott, Hoch, and Stetler, p. 368.

194. 13 H 183; CD 85.64: Richard L. Clark, narcotics and vice squad, SSB, "has contacted Ruby on investigative matters on an average of once a month."

195. CD 732, CD 1052 (letters from J. Edgar Hoover to J. Lee Rankin, April 7, 1964, June 9, 1964); discussed in Paul L. Hoch, *The Oswald Papers: The FBI Versus the Warren Commission,* unpublished manuscript, II.A.4.

196. Chicago Crime Commission, 1965 Report, p. 81.

197. Congressional Record, April 15, 1954, p. 5238.

198. Jack Lait and Lee Mortimer, *USA Confidential* (New York: Crown, 1952), p. 197 (Clark-Nichols); 22 H 506 (Ruby); *Fortune,* February 1953, p. 232 (Murchison-Nichols).

199. Michael Dorman, *Vesco: The Infernal Money Making Machine* (New York: Berkley Medallion Books, 1975), pp. 53-65; cf. McClellan Hearings, p. 12520. On December 30, 1968, the airline, then known as Texas International Airlines, acquired the Las Vegas Tropicana, whose sellers had been represented by Edward P. Morgan (20 Wat 9498, cf. 24 Wat 11416).

199a. Dorman, p. 57; 23 H 157, 26 H 650, CD 441.

200. Ovid Demaris, *The Director* (New York: Harper's Magazine Press, 1975), p. 15 (Del Charro); Anderson, *Washington Expose,* pp. 214-16 (Eisenhower). Clint Murchison and Robert Thompson (involved in the Webb-Baker payoff) were leading members of the Del Charro set.

201. 25 H 244; McClellan Hearings, p. 14072 (Harriman).

202. 23 H 374, 5 H 200, 14 H 446; *New York Times,* June 29, 1976, p. 16.

203. 25 H 244; cf. Ruby at 5 H 200 ("Deutsch I. Maylor"), Scott in Scott, Hoch and Stetler, p. 370.

204. U.S., Cong., Senate, Committee on Government Operations, *American Guild of Variety Artists, Hearings,* 87th Cong., 2nd Sess. (Washington: Govern-

ment Printing Office, 1962). The Committee heard that AGVA solicited girls from Havana for work as strippers and b-girls (p. 287); Ruby is also rumored to have solicited girls from Havana and to have operated a strippers' school in Dallas.

205. 23 H 33, 25 H 284; cf. 23 H 53, 15 H 207-17.

206. Sheridan, pp. 236, 274, 406-408. Chavez, who allegedly first tried to kill Robert Kennedy in 1964, was also implicated by one source in the John F. Kennedy assassination (Sheridan, p. 407; CD 301.66, cf. 26 H 472).

207. Sheridan, pp. 503-506. Lester May was earlier the attorney for Juanita Phillips or "Candy Barr," porno film star and friend of Jack Ruby and Mickey Cohen: Gary Wills and Ovid Demaris, *Jack Ruby* (New York: New American Library, 1967), p. 68; cf. 23 H 98. After Phillips was convicted on a narcotics charge, Mickey Cohen brought in Mel Belli (who was later Ruby's defense attorney) to appeal the verdict.

208. 25 H 246; Sheridan, p. 492; McClellan Hearings, p. 17217; Congressional Record, 1970, p. 27751. A "Nofie" Pecoraro, aged twenty-eight, was arrested in 1934 in a guns-for-arms smuggling case involving Honduras; Maurice Helbrant, *Narcotic Agents* (New York: Vanguard, 1941), pp. 265-81.

209. *Los Angeles Times,* September 12, 1970; 22 H 329. Cf. Stolen Securities Hearings, pp. 688, 684, 850, 854, 856, 870 (for Emil Tucker, indicted with Smith and Medlevine), p. 713 (Beckley), p. 853 (Marcello), p. 854 (Tourine, p. 713 (McLaney); p. 713 (Benton).

Maurice Medlevine's brother Donald, another Miller gang member and friend of Jack Ruby, managed the Chez Paree in Chicago for Charles "the Babe" Baron, Lansky's casino representative in Havana and an Arvey family associate in Havana (22 H 319; Demaris, *Captive City,* p. 249; supra at note 180). As references for Ruby's background, Don Medlevine suggested Dave "Dingy" Halper, Baron's associate at the Las Vegas Riviera casino (an alleged Giancana investment; *Playboy,* March 1972, p. 172) and Jay Schatz, the manager of Gordon McLendon's station WYNR in Chicago (22 H 319, cf. 25 H 228).

210. Peter Dale Scott, "Vietnamization and the Drama of the Pentagon Papers," in Noam Chomsky and Howard Zinn, eds., *Pentagon Papers Volume V: Critical Essays* (Boston: Beacon Press, 1972), pp. 211-47; excerpted in Scott, Hoch, and Stetler, pp. 406-42; cf. Scott, in Blumenthal and Yazijian, pp. 152-87.

211. Peter Dale Scott, "The Vietnam War and the CIA-Financial Establishment," in Mark Selden, ed., *Remaking Asia: Essays on the American Use of Power* (New York: Pantheon, 1974), pp. 107-111.

212. Demaris, *Dirty Business,* pp. 84-85.

213. Demaris, pp. 215-22; Christopher T. Rand, *Making Democracy Safe for Oil: Oilmen and the Islamic East* (Boston: Atlantic, Little, Brown, 1975), pp. 322-31. In December 1973, the Shah of Iran told reporters, in an unpublished press conference whose transcript he later published in the *New York Times* as a full-page advertisement, that "the oil companies . . . raised the price of oil to what it is now, that is, $9.74. I did not do it. The oil companies did." (Rand, p. 323; *New York Times,* November 11, 1974)

214. Thus Robert Maheu only became famous after he ceased earning

$500,000 a year from the Hughes operations; and few have heard of the comparable ex-FBI agency chief (M. B. Leckie) who helped displace him.

215. "A government source recently complained to me that Exxon's Venezuelan subsidiary, Creole, Inc., has a larger intelligence budget than the local CIA station—and that, in recognition of this, the organizations have consolidated their files: in Venezuela, at least, what's good for Creole is apparently good for America" (Jim Hougan, "A Surfeit of Spies," *Harper's,* December 1974, p. 53). Former U.S. ambassador to Colombia Spruille Braden recalled that in the 1930s the embassy's only intelligence resources were those supplied by the local subsidiaries of Standard of California and Texaco: U.S., Cong., Senate, Committee on the Judiciary, *Communist Threat to the United States Through the Caribbean, Hearings,* 86th Cong., 1st Sess. (Washington: Government Printing Office, 1959), p. 283; cf. Scott, in Selden, pp. 128, 150; Scott, in Caldwell, pp. 225-27.

216. Scott, *War Conspiracy,* p. 171.

Index

About the Author

Peter Dale Scott was born in 1929 in Montreal, Canada. A former Canadian diplomat with a Ph.D. in political science, he now teaches English at the University of California, Berkeley. In addition to poetry and translations of poetry, he has published on topics ranging from medieval literature to the origins of the Vietnam War. While writing a book-length study of the latter (*The War Conspiracy*, 1972), he discovered important shifts in U.S. Vietnam policy that followed within forty-eight hours of the assassination of President John F. Kennedy. Since 1972 he has continued to research and publish on the political context of the Kennedy assassination. Three of his essays in that area are included in the anthology *The Assassinations—Dallas and Beyond* (1976), of which he was co-editor.